Faith
and Freedom -
The Scots-Irish
in America

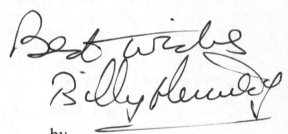

by
BILLY KENNEDY

AMBASSADOR

Belfast Northern Ireland **Greenville** South Carolina

Faith and Freedom - The Scots-Irish in America
© 1999 Billy Kennedy

First published September, 1999

THE SCOTS-IRISH CHRONICLES

The Scots-Irish in the Hills of Tennessee (published 1995)
The Scots-Irish in the Shenandoah Valley (published 1996)
The Scots-Irish in the Carolinas (published 1997)
The Scots-Irish in Pennsylvania and Kentucky (published 1998)
Faith and Freedom - The Scots-Irish in America (published 1999)

PRINTED IN NORTHERN IRELAND

Published by

Causeway Press

Ambassador Productions Ltd.,
Providence House
16 Hillview Avenue,
Belfast, BT5 6JR

Emerald House Group Inc.
1 Chick Springs Road, Suite 206
Greenville, South Carolina, 29609

About *the Author*

This is BILLY KENNEDY's fifth book in five years on the Scots-Irish settlements in America in the 18th century and all have been extensively researched on both sides of the Atlantic. Billy Kennedy, born in 1943 and resident in Co Armagh, Northern Ireland for almost the entire period of his life, comes from an Ulster-Scots Presbyterian background. He is a journalist of wide recognition over a period of more than 30 years, having had a role as assistant editor and leader writer for five years and a news editor for eighteen years with the Ulster-Belfast News Letter, the main morning newspaper in Northern Ireland, founded in 1737. He now works as a free-lance journalist, public relations consultant and author, combining news, feature and sports coverage in Northern Ireland for press and media outlets. He combines a deep interest in the Scots-Irish diaspora in the United States and, through his authorship, Billy Kennedy has lectured on the subject of the Scots-Irish at universities, colleges, historical societies and public authorities in cities and towns of the south eastern American states. He is an authority on American country music and culture, travels to Nashville regularly and has interviewed for the Ulster-Belfast News Letter many of the top singing stars. He is also a specialist on sport, politics and religious affairs. His sporting connections are mainly in soccer and since 1973 he has been a member of the board of management of Linfield, Ireland's leading soccer club. He has also compiled and edited books on sport, religion and cultural traditions in Ireland, including two on the Orange Order. He is married with a grown-up daughter.

Dedication

This book is dedicated to my loving wife Sally,
daughter Julie and my parents.

"But you are a chosen generation, a royal priesthood, an holy nation,
a peculiar people; that ye should shew forth the praises of Him who
hath called you out of darkness into His marvellous light. Which in
time past were not a people, but are now the people of God; which had
not obtained mercy, but now have obtained mercy."
FIRST PETER, chapter 2, verses 9-10.

The author acknowledges the help and support given to him in the
compilation of this book by Samuel Lowry, of Ambassador
Productions/Causeway Press, and Tomm Knutson, of Emerald House,
Greenville, South Carolina.

List *of contents*

Cover illustration

The statue of General Andrew Jackson, the victorious commander of the American forces at the Battle of New Orleans in January, 1815, a battle which effectively ended British influence in the southern states and settled some of the land disputes with the native Indian tribes. The famous statue is situated in the dome of the Capitol Building in Washington DC and the picture appears with consent from the United States government authorities.

The New Orleans triumph made Andrew Jackson the most popular man in America at the time and it acted as the springboard for him to make it to the White House for two terms as President. Jackson's direct adversary at the Battle of New Orleans was British general Sir Edward Packenham, a soldier trained in the classic European school of warfare. It was said that Packenham was rudely awakened by the unorthodox fighting methods of Jackson's Tennesseans and other troops in the Louisiana swamplands and he himself was killed in conflict.

Years later, Jackson recalled: "I heard a single rifle shot from a group of country carts we had been using, and a moment thereafter I saw Packenham reel and pitch out of his saddle. I did not know where General Packenham was lying or I should have sent to him, or gone to him in person, to offer any service in my power to render. I was told he lived two hours after he was hit."

Andrew Jackson, of course, was born in the Waxhaws area in 1767 on the state line between North Carolina and South Carolina, his Presbyterian linen weaver parents Andrew and Elizabeth Jackson having left Boneybefore near Carrickfergus, Co Antrim in the north of Ireland for America eighteen months earlier.

Thanks

I would again gratefully acknowledge the tremendous help and assistance given to me by so many people in the United States in the preparation and compilation of my five books on the Scots-Irish Presbyterian settlements on the American frontier during the 18th and early 19th centuries. I have received a vast amount of help and information on families, personalities and events of the Scots-Irish tradition and culture and I really appreciate the time and effort taken by people over a wide area of the United States. Like me, they are immensely proud of the outstanding achievements of their forebears, whose pioneering spirit and exploits helped make the United States the great nation that it is today. With great valour and a work ethic that set them apart, the Scots-Irish stamped their unique character on the constitution and religious, cultural and social landscape of America. They were indeed a very special people and for posterity their outstanding exploits are recorded on these pages.

BILLY KENNEDY

The author can be contacted at:
49, Knockview Drive,
Tandragee,
Craigavon,
Co Armagh,
Northern Ireland BT62 2BH.

Foreword *from the United States*

Dr. John Rice Irwin

T his is the fifth book Billy Kennedy has written concerning the colorful and stalwart Scots-Irish in America and the incredible influence they had on the settlement and development of this great nation over a period of several centuries.

Billy, a fast moving, energetic newspaperman who writes for the Ulster-Belfast News Letter and other media and press outlets in Northern Ireland, is a prodigious worker and one with an insatiable interest in "his" people after they came to America from the north of Ireland generations ago. And the more he learns of their role in building America, the more titillated and inspired he becomes.

His first book, The Scots-Irish in the Hills of Tennessee, was followed by The Scots-Irish in the Shenandoah Valley, then The Scots-Irish in the Carolinas and his fourth book was titled The Scots-Irish in Pennsylvania and Kentucky.

For each of these I wrote a foreword, bringing forth the good and appropriate thoughts and observations with regard to Billy's mission. Now comes this, the fifth (and he says the last!) in the series of Scots-Irish Chronicles. So without being repetitious or redundant, I set forth the following general comments with respect to this volume.

First, I'm convinced that the favorable stir created in this country by his earlier books on the Scots-Irish will be rekindled by this one. Faith and Freedom - The Scots-Irish in America. Perhaps no two words could more aptly characterise the Scots-Irish.

They were fervent and exemplary in their demonstration of faith and faithfulness and of their love of freedom; and these characteristics influenced the people of this country and imbued them with a sense of intense pride, honesty and loyalty to their Presbyterian form of religion and to the state as well.

While Billy's other books have concentrated on a detailed study of the enormous contributions and impact, both individually and collectively, that the Scots-Irish have had on certain regions in this country, Faith and Freedom - The Scots-Irish in America is not confined to a specific geographic area, but rather it relates to the great eastern and southern part of the United States, from New Hampshire to Mississippi and down to Texas and Louisiana.

Literally hundreds of people, places and historical events related to the Scots-Irish are mentioned and discussed in this volume; and from any one of these entries, a reader on this side of the Atlantic could launch an exhaustive and interesting foray into the highly colorful and fascinating days of one's ancestry.

Billy Kennedy has turned over a thousand stones, each revealing, just enough suggestive treasure trove of the past to cause curious and analytical people to be pleasurably excited and motivated to delve in with a vengeance to learn more of one's past - of one's self.

DR JOHN RICE IRWIN,
Director of Museum of Appalachia, Norris, Tennessee.

• **Dr John Rice Irwin** is founder and director of the Museum of Appalachia at Norris, Tennessee, 15 miles from the city of Knoxville. This East Tennessee farm village has gained national and international recognition for its concentration on the rich culture and folklore of the Appalachian mountain region. Dr Irwin has been a teacher, farmer, businessman, historian, author and his wide range of interests also extends to the music of his south eastern home region. His family is of 18th century Scots-Irish and Welsh extraction.

Scene from the Museum of Appalachia, East Tennessee

MODERN
IRELAND

ULSTER

Coleraine
Londonderry
Larne
Ballymena
Donegal
Omagh
Belfast
Enniskillen
Downpatrick
Sligo
Armagh
Newry
Ballina
Cavan
Dundalk
Castlebar
Drogheda
Roscommon
Clifden
Athlone
Dublin
Dun Laoghaire
Galway
Portlaoise
Wicklow
Roscrea
Arklow
Ennis
Kilkee
Limerick
Kilkenny
Tipperary
Clonmel
Wexford
Tralee
Waterford
Rosslare
Killarney
Cork
Bantry

Foreword *from Northern Ireland*

Cllr. Dr. Ian Adamson OBE

Billy Kennedy's SCOTS-IRISH CHRONICLES detail the major impact Ulster settlers made in the birth of the United States and in this latest book he shows that Ulster's heritage is not confined to Ireland, but has much broader significance.

In his fifth book 'Faith and Freedom', Billy has concentrated on the radical thinking which culminated so dramatically in the formation of a new world. One of the most important influences in its development was the work of the great Ulster philosopher, Frances Hutcheson, son of an Armagh Presbyterian minister, who was born probably at Drumalig, Saintfield, Co Down, in 1694.

Frances Hutcheson studied for the Church at Glasgow University (1710-1716), but then started a private academy in Dublin where he was particularly associated with the advanced Presbyterian libertarian thinkers - Thomas Drennan, William Bruce and Samuel Halliday.

In 1729, Hutcheson was appointed Professor of Moral Philosophy at Glasgow, where he died in 1746. His most important work is 'A Sense of Moral Philosophy' and in it he was quite explicit about the right of resistance by the people in the event of betrayal by a government. Hutcheson expounded the doctrine of religious toleration and he deeply admired the tradition of armed militias for the protection of civil liberties. The principles he espoused found their way via American revolutionary thinkers into the Declaration of Independence and are embodied in the American constitution.

Hutcheson's influence on Presidents Thomas Jefferson and John Adams and other prominent leaders is explored in the books Philosophy of the American Revolution by M. White and Inventing American by G. Willis. In fact, Willis concluded that Hutcheson's influence on Jefferson was stronger than that of noted English philosopher John Locke.

The official Declaration of Independence was written in the hand-writing of Charles Thomson, from Maghera, Co Londonderry; printed by John Dunlap, from Strabane, Co Tyrone; given its first reading by the son of an Ulsterman Colonel John Nixon and among the signatories were the following, all either born in Ulster, or born to Ulster parents - John Hancock (President of Congress), Thomas McKean, Thomas Nelson, Robert Baine, Edward Rutledge, George Taylor, Matthew Thornton and William Whipple.

The Great Seal of the United States - an eagle holding an arrow and a branch - was designed by Charles Thomson after a Congressional Committee, consisting of Benjamin Franklin and John Adams, broke up in disagreement.

Edward Rutledge's brother John, chaired a committee of five states which drew up the United States Constitution. According to historian Alexis de Tocqueville, the United States Constitution bore Rutledge's "personal stamp." He said: "One man made it and it was Rutledge."

Yet, it is extremely ironic when viewed from today's perspective that, in America, the Scots-Irish, who were largely Ulster Presbyterian in origin, would throw themselves wholeheartedly into the republican camp, believing that an independent American republic was eminently more desirable for their social and economic well-being than continued control and interference by Britain.

However, the growing economic and political power of these new republicans proved threatening to other sections of American society, who stayed decidedly loyalist, including many Roman Catholic Jacobites from the Highlands of Scotland, who had fought the House of Hanover in the 1745 Rebellion and remembered the defeat in the first Scottish Rising of 1715, but who became staunch Loyalists because of the generous treatment they received in America from their former adversaries.

Various cultural minorities, fearful of an increase in the power of the majority, often sought British help or protection. New Rochelle, for example, the only place where the French Calvinists still spoke French, was an area of substantial Huguenot Loyalism.

Nor were America's Black population convinced that an alliance with radical republicans was really to their advantage. Most of the Black community were "strongly attached to the British", according to one contemporary Loyalist source.

Certainly, there was a widespread fear of Black people among the newly consolidating American Establishment, partly an extension of the perennial dread of slave revolt and intensified by the mass desertion of slaves in response to a wholesale British offer of freedom.

Indeed, a strong disapproval of Black slavery was the most glaring omission from the Declaration of Independence. Matthew T. Mellon, of the great American banking family which itself derived from Castletown near Omagh in Co Tyrone, concluded in his study of the racial attitudes of America's founding fathers, 'Early American Views of Negro Slavery', that while the leading men at the time of the Revolution were all concerned with how to abolish the slave trade, economic pressures and moral indifference prevented them from energetically pursuing its abolition.

As the American Revolution gained momentum, the Indian peoples made some attempt at neutrality, but generally they favoured the British Government also. They had no enthusiasm for the westward pushing, uncontrollable Scots-Irish settlers who coveted their lands. The Indians believed that the British, rather than the Americans, would be the most likely to seek restraints over this movement.

Nothing highlights this allegiance better than the careers of the prominent loyalists who emerged among the Mohawk people, such as John Deserontyon, Aaron Hill and Joseph Grant, who commanded the Iroquois Indian nations with great skill on the British side during the Revolutionary War.

Yet where would we be today if it were not for the popular democracy initiated by the American Revolution? Where would we be today if that conglomerate of ancient peoples known to us as the Scots-Irish had not left their Ulster homeland to fight for faith and freedom on American lands? - and where, indeed, would we be today if we did not have such a fine journalist as Billy Kennedy to tell the story?

COUNCILLOR DR. IAN ADAMSON OBE.
Member of the Northern Ireland Assembly
for constituency of East Belfast.
Former Lord Mayor of Belfast.

Books by Dr. Ian Adamson:

- The Cruthin (1974)
- Bangor, Light of the World (1979)
- The Battle of Moira (1980)
- The Identity of Ulster (1982)
- The Ulster People (1991)

1

Witnessing for *Faith and Freedom*

Faith and freedom have been eternal watchwords from the very beginning of man and for the doughty Scots-Irish Presbyterian people who emigrated to America during the 18th century these were the cherished ideals that kept them going as they moved in the 17th century Plantation years over the short sea journey from Scotland to Ulster, and then made the the the long trek across the Atlantic for the adventure into the great unknown of the frontier lands of the 'New World'.

The God-fearing Scots-Irish combined in their ideals: a total reverence for the Almighty, deep devotion to their families, sincere love of country and a passionate belief in their liberty. Individuals may have strayed from the paths of these convictions, but generally as a people the Scots-Irish stayed true to the four cornerstones of life: God, country, family and liberty.

Establishing a settlement in the harsh, rugged and, in parts, hostile countryside of the north of Ireland during the 17th century prepared the Scots-Irish for their experiences when they arrived in America to start a new life. By the time they reached America, the Scots-Irish had survived wars, sieges, famine, drought and religious persecution. They were certainly not deterred by the dangers they faced in their new environment and most found the wide open spaces of America to their liking.

Indeed, largely due to their past experiences in lowland Scotland and the north of Ireland, the Scots-Irish fared much better than the other white ethnic groups like the English, Germans, Welsh, Dutch,

Scottish Highlanders, Swiss and Scandinavians in resisting the hostilities of the native American tribes; in fending off English, French and Spanish colonial predators and oppressors and pushing the frontier south and west to its very outer limits.

The Scots-Irish effectively set the parameters for life in many cities and towns established along the western frontier of 18th century America and, with their close identification to church, school and the home, they were able to lay the foundations for a civilised society which placed total emphasis on a belief in God and in the value of liberty of conscience and democracy.

The work ethic and commitment to a cause by the Scots-Irish is best summed up in these words of celebrated Ulster historian, folklorist and Co Tyrone Presbyterian cleric the Rev W. F. Marshall: "The Scots-Irish were the first to start and the last to quit." The vigour and grit of the race were seen in their pioneering instinct.

Three hundred years have past since the first Ulster-Scots immigrants such as Co Donegal Presbyterian pastor Francis Makemie landed on American soil and, in that time, the enormous landscape of the United States has changed beyond all recognition, with the political, social and cultural perspectives of the population now increasingly diverse in the great melting pot of humanity.

The fundamentals of Faith and Freedom so profound, meaningful and enriching to these proud pioneering people from Ulster and lowland Scotland have been permanently ingrained in the constitutional imperatives of the American nation and, today, they stand testimony to all that was achieved in the early formative years of struggle and supreme sacrifice on the frontier.

The Declaration of Independence of July 4, 1776, which Ulstermen helped draw up, contained fine Christian sentiments: "We hold these truths to be self-evident, that all men are created equal, that they are endowed by their Creator with certain inalienable rights, that among them are life, liberty and the pursuit of happiness."

The distinctive characteristics which the Scots-Irish brought to America in the 18th century were very accurately identified by late 19th century historian John Patterson MacLean, who said: "They were Presbyterian in religion and church government; they were loyal to the conceded authority to the King, but considered him bound as well as themselves to the Solemn League and Covenant entered into in 1643, which pledged the support of the Protestant Reformation and the liberties of the Kingdom; the right to choose their own ministers, untrammelled by the civil powers.

"They practiced strict discipline in morals and gave instruction to the youth in their schools and academies, and in teaching the Bible as illustrated by the Westminster Confession of Faith. To all this combined in a remarkable degree, acuteness of intellect, firmness of purpose and conscientious devotion to duty."

From Pennsylvania through the Shenandoah Valley of Virginia to North Carolina, South Carolina, Tennessee, Georgia and Kentucky; on to the territories of Mississippi, Louisiana, Texas, Oklahoma, Kansas, Nevada, Colorado and California, the Scots-Irish settlers blazed the pioneering trail in America for others to follow. They were a durable determined people with the special personal stamp needed to tame the wilds of the frontier and make it a place habitable for civilised family life.

Between 1717 and the end of the 18th century an estimated quarter of a million Scots-Irish Presbyterians emigrated to the United States from Ulster. In simple wooden sailing ships they sailed from the ports of Belfast, Larne, Londonderry, Portrush and Newry for the far-flung berths of New York, Philadelphia, New Castle (Delaware), Boston, Baltimore and Charleston.

In the United States today an estimated 44 million people claim Irish extraction and, of these folk, 56 per cent are Protestant stock, whose forebears were Scots-Irish Presbyterians who settled on the American frontier in the 18th century. Scots-Irish influence is far-reaching in the United States.

Scots-Irish ingenuity

The land of cotton in the South extends from Virginia and Tennessee through to Georgia, Mississippi, Louisiana, Alabama and Arkansas and west to Texas. The cotton plant has prehistoric and international origins and it is believed to have been cultivated in Mexico as far back as 5000 BC, and in India 3000 BC.

In 1792, inventor Eli Whitney from Connecticut built and patented a cotton gin (seeder) on a Georgian plantation which revolutionised the industry. Because of Whitney's gin, cotton production in the American South increased from 138,000 pounds in 1792 to 35,000,000 pounds in 1800.

A few years later, Tennessean John McBride, a man of Scots-Irish family roots, went further with the invention of a cotton gin spinner. This machine not only took the seed from the cotton fibre, but also carded and spun the fibre into thread. The first McBride cotton gin spinner is believed to have been erected in 1805 on the lands of President Andrew Jackson at The Hermitage near Nashville.

2

Scots-Irish *origins, terminology and ambitions*

Population movement in both directions between Scotland and the north of Ireland has gone on for most of 2,000 years. The sea journey between the Ulster coastline and the western parts of Scotland is at its shortest 15 miles and longest 50 miles, and at most the peoples of the two countries are never more than a day's sailing away from each other.

Scholars confirm that the name Scotland was never applied to that country before the tenth century. It was called Alban or Albion and in that period the geographical and territorial term for Ireland was Scotia. Scotus was the race or generic term.

From about 500 AD, Dalriadic Scots, operating in the north eastern part of Ireland around Co Antrim under the leadership of Fergus McErc and his brothers Lorne and Angus, left Ireland to settle in Argyllshire and the western isles of Scotland. From Fergus was derived the line of Scoto-Irish kings and for centuries the inhabitants of the highlands of Scotland shared a common bond and language similarities.

The advent of the Protestant Reformation caused major strains between the ruling authorities and populations in the two countries, with people in Scotland by and large opting for a strongly non-conformist Calvinist doctrine as advocated by John Calvin in Geneva and John Knox in Edinburgh, and the inhabitants of Ireland sticking by the old Catholic faith, as dictated from Rome.

From the mid-16th century, Presbyterian ministers renounced the right of interference by the civil magistrates, "whether subject or sovereign", in the affairs of the church. They also discarded the subordination of ministerial ranks, maintaining that each minister be entrusted with the charge of souls.

A plantation strategy was drawn up by 17th century British monarch James 1 (James V1 of Scotland) and, with half a million acres of land at his disposal over most of the Province of Ulster, he set about establishing English and Scottish colonies in Ireland, with the chief seat of colonisation Londonderry.

The 17th Scottish plantation concentrated in large parts of counties Antrim, Down, Tyrone, Londonderry and Donegal. An English plantation of Ireland had begun in the late 16th century and, while it extended over the entire part of the island, its Ulster influence centred more in counties Armagh and Fermanagh.

The Proclamation inviting Scottish settlers to move to Ulster was dated at Edinburgh on March 29, 1609 and the planter stock was recruited mainly from the strongly Presbyterian shires and burghs of Glasgow, Renfrew, Lanark, Dumbarton, Ayr, Dumfries, Argyll, Galloway and the Lothians.

Scottish soldiers serving in the north of Ireland during the early 17th century and their families boosted the numbers in the plantation colonies and army chaplains in Scottish regiments played a primary role in the formation of the Presbyterian Church in the cities and towns of Ulster for several decades from about 1610.

The first presbytery of the Presbyterian Church in Ireland was constituted at Carrickfergus, Co Antrim (the home of President Andrew Jackson's parents) on June 10, 1642 by chaplains and officers of Scottish regiments based in that town. The five chaplains who attended were the Rev Hugh Cunningham, the Rev Thomas Peebles, the Rev John Scott, the Rev John Baird and the Rev John Aird. Baird was appointed moderator and Peebles clerk of presbytery.

The Scottish regiments, under Major General Robert Monro, were in Ulster to quell a rebellion by the native Irish Roman Catholics against the Protestant population and Presbyterian chaplains were attached to each regiment. Many of these clerics stayed in the north of Ireland to take up ministerial posts. The church had by then branched out from first locations in East Antrim, North Down and Londonderry to take in virtually all the nine counties of Ulster.

The flame from the Presbyterian burning bush symbol was burning brightly. By 1654, five presbyteries were functioning in Down, Carrickfergus in East Antrim, the Route area of North Antrim, Laggan in Donegal-Londonderry and Tyrone, and new congregations were sprouting up all over the Province.

In 1688, the Presbyterians of Ulster sided with the Dutch Protestant king William of Orange against the Roman Catholic James II and they formed themselves into county associations so as to take "the most decisive and effective steps" to secure themselves against what they considered the "vindictive measures" of James's lieutenant Lord Tyrconnell.

The Presbyterians were heavily involved in the defence of the walled city of Londonderry during the Siege of 1688-89 and many of their number fought with William of Orange at the Battle of the Boyne in 1690, a battle which led to the Glorious Revolution confirming the Protestant succession on the throne of England.

The reign of William of Orange ended in 1702 and, when his cousin Anne ascended the throne, High Anglican churchmen in the government of the day in London enacted laws which bore down mightily on the minds and consciences of the Ulster Presbyterian planter stock.

An Act was passed in 1703 which required all office-bearers of the Crown in Ireland to take the Established Episcopal sacraments. Many Presbyterians in positions of magistrates and civil servants were automatically disqualified unless their renounced their Calvinist faith. Many were turned out of their pulpits.

Ministers were told their Presbyterian ordinances were null and void; they could no longer officiate at baptisms, marriages and burials and they were prevented from teaching on any aspect of their faith and doctrine.

The seeds of social unrest were sown throughout a large section of the Ulster community and, increasingly, many Presbyterians began to focus on the prospects of a new life in the America colonies where they could be assured of the necessary space for the propagation of their faith and freedom.

The economic situation in the north of Ireland at that time also played a part in persuading many people to emigrate to America. Agriculture was the main industry in the Ulster of the mid-18th century and, with basic implements to toil and harvest the farmlands, it was a far from reliable source of income.

The trek across the Atlantic had begun in earnest and the trickle of disaffected Ulster-Scots Presbyterians to the far-off lands became a flood in the 100 years that followed. Ulster was indeed to lose many of its best citizens, but America was to benefit immeasurably from their enterprise and toil and, in the moulding of a new nation, these hardy immigrants played no small part.

* Scottish highlanders, a large percentage of whom were Roman Catholics operating a clan system, did not join in any significant numbers the plantation trail to Ulster, even though they had a direct blood line with the native Irish people there, particularly in the Co Antrim glens, dating back for more than 1,000 years.

> *"The generic term of Scoti embraced the people of that race whether inhabiting Ireland or Britain. As this term of Scotia was a geographical term derived from the generic name of a people, it was to some extent a fluctuating name, and though applied at first to Ireland, which possessed the more distinctive name of Hibernia, as the principal seat of the race from whom the name was derived, it is obvious, that if the people from whom the name was taken inhabited other countries, the name itself would have a tendency to pass from one to the other, according to the prominence which the different settlements of the race assumed in the history of the world.*
>
> *And as the race of the Scots in Britain became more extended, and their power more formidable, the territorial name would have a tendency to fix itself where the race had become most conspicuous. The name in its Latin form of Scotia was transferred from Ireland to Scotland in the reign of Malcolm the Second (1004-1034).*
>
> *The 'Pictish Chronicle', compiled before 997, knows nothing of Scotia as applied to North Britain; but Marianus Scotus, who lived from 1028 to 1081, called Malcolm the Second 'rex Scotiae', and Brian, king of Ireland, 'rex Hiberniae'. The author of the 'Life of St Cadroe', in the eleventh century, likewise applied the name of Scotia to North Britain."*

From Skene's 'CHRONICLES of the PICTS and SCOTS'.

3

Perilous journey *to a new land*

The journey across the Atlantic from Ulster to America in the 18th century took an average period of six to eight weeks, depending on the weather and the sea worthiness of the vessel. But the arrival at an American port did not automatically mean passengers could embark ship immediately. The quarantine laws had to be strictly observed and passengers were often forced to remain on board for weeks until the danger from disease and infection had passed.

Serious overcrowding and lack of food and fresh water were the main complaints of those who travelled on the immigrant ships, both paying passengers and indentured servants. The weather forced many passengers to remain below deck for long periods and it was there, in the steamy atmosphere of the confined spaces, that exposure to the fatal diseases lay.

Child mortality was common on the journey, but illness also took its toll of adults and when death came the bodies were thrown overboard after the appropriate burial rights were observed. It is remarkable, however, that of the hundreds of thousands of 18th century Ulster emigrants who set out for America in the numerous wooden sailing ships, only a very small percentage perished before completing the journey.

A large proportion of Atlantic journeys were completed with the minimum of fuss. Indeed, the greatest hardships of the passengers on board some ships were said to be boredom and discomfort. But such was the harshness of conditions for many people on the Ulster hillsides in the 18th century that they were happy to put with some deprivation and suffering to obtain freedom and a better deal in the New World.

The emigrant ships normally sailed in the spring, summer and autumn - a mid-winter journey across the Atlantic was not advisable. Weather predictions in those days were somewhat hazy and very often ship captains threw caution to the wind in venturing out into the unknown.

Heavy trans-Atlantic storms caused shipwreck for some vessels, but those which did not reach their destination were the exception rather than the rule. It was generally accepted that the Ulster shipowners and captains had a much better safety and success record than their counterparts from German, Dutch and French ports who ferried the German Palatine Lutheran immigrants to America.

Ships carrying German immigrants in the early part of the 18th century were often ravaged by typhus, a disease that became commonly known at the time as the 'Palatine fever'. On one German vessel eighty people died before the journey began, and on another 330 were afflicted by typhus over the duration of the journey.

Emigration agents in Ulster always presented a positive opinion on the transatlantic voyage and accounts rarely mentioned sickness or death. Fever thrived on overcrowding and during the years of heavy emigration sickness was prevalent.

Thousands emigrated in 1741-42 at the time of the famine in Ireland and the then Governor of Pennsylvania, George Thomas asked his assembly to set up a hospital or rest house to accommodate sick immigrants. Irish and German immigrants, in that order, were specified as being in most need of attention.

Smallpox was reported on at least two ships that sailed from Larne in 1772 and passengers on two Newry ships bound for Charleston were reported to be "remarkably sick". A number died during the crossing.

4

Early Scots-Irish settlements
on the Delaware River

White Clay Presbyterian Church at New Castle, Delaware was founded by Scots-Irish settlers who arrived in the earliest 18th century immigrant ships from Ulster. White Clay had originally been a Dutch Reformed church, but by 1721 the congregation was dominated by Scots-Irish families and moulded in their distinctive character and spiritual witness.

William McMechen and his family from Newry in Co Down arrived at New Castle some time between 1718 and 1721 and with others from Ulster they set up home at White Clay Creek and enrolled at the Presbyterian church. The minister there from 1723 was the Rev Thomas Craighead, who was also an extensive land-owner acquiring 402 acres of land some of which he sold in 1727 to members of his congregation including William McMechen.

Close by in the village of Christiana, there was a Presbyterian church of which William McMechen was an elder before his move to White Clay and at the time the region was inhabited by a mixture of Ulster-Scots, Welsh, English and German-Dutch peoples.

William McMechen and his Irish-born wife Janette had six sons and a daughter, but when Janette died in 1734 William married a second time to Rebecca.

The couple were only several years together when William passed on in 1738. Interestingly, William's estate on his death was valued at £170-18-3, a sizeable sum for the period.

His eldest son James was a formidable public figure, being a justice of the peace and a member of the Pennsylvanian assembly. He served as a lieutenant with the White Clay Creek regiments in the French and Indian war of 1754-63 and like his father was an elder in the Presbyterian Church.

White Clay meeting house was a typical early 18th century structure and, after Thomas Craighead, the pastor was the Rev Charles Tennent, son of the Rev William Tennent, who soon after his arrival from Ireland had become renowned for his "log college" ministerial training institution.

William Tennent was a Presbyterian visionary whose main mission in life was to ordain ministers on American soil for there were not enough clerics with the theological background from the 'Old World' to keep up with the increasing demand as more and more frontier churches were established.

George Whitefield, the noted English evangelist, had the first of a number of preaching engagements at White Clay Creek in 1739 and, while his presence and proselytising work was opposed by some conservative Presbyterians accustomed to 'Old World' theology, he worked closely with William Tennent to the saving of many souls.

A deep split occurred in 1741 and for 20 years there were two White Clay congregations, divided along 'New Side' and 'Old Side' interpretations of the faith. James McMechen and his family were attached to the 'New Side' group.

William McMechen, a son of James, moved from New Castle county, Delaware and he was one of earliest settlers in modern-day Marshall county in West Virginia, today centred on the town of Wheeling.

Dr James McMechen, a brother, accompanied him in the arduous journey over the Blue Ridge Mountain to seek new lands and in 1771 they settled along the Ohio River in a region George Washington actively surveyed in the years following the French-Indian War.

It is recorded that the equipment of William and James McMechen for such an unknown and adventurous journey was a modest one. They merely packed all their provisions on a couple of pack horses, but were armed for defence with flintlocks and tomahawks. They kept on the ridges of the mountain to avoid the straggling bands of Indians who were giving the white settlers so much trouble.

The quality of life for first frontier settlers like the McMechen brothers was extremely precarious and, constantly, they had to look over their shoulders for fear of Indian attacks, with the tribesmen either intent on stealing horses and cattle or halting the white families in their relentless westward trek. John Boyd, a close associate of Dr James McMechen, was murdered in one of these attacks in 1774 and the situation worsened during the Revolutionary War when Indians, acting in collusion with British forces, killed and injured many of the pro-independence settlers.

William McMechen was a revolutionary captain in the Virginia militia and he was present at the defence of Fort Henry on September 1, 1777 when many died in a ferocious Indian attack. Later that month, 21 militiamen were killed in an ambush on William McMechen's West Virginia property by a band of Indians under Half King, a Wyandot chief.

McMechen's cabins and outbuildings were twice burned down by Indians and he had to remove his family to the safety of the Red Stone Old Fort at Brownsville in Fayette county, Pennsylvania, where they stayed for two years until 1782 when the danger had subsided.

Hostilities simmered in these north-west territories for another decade and relative peace came about after forces under General Anthony Wayne defeated the Indians at Fallen Timbers in August, 1794 and the Treaty of Greenville was signed which forced the tribes to cede almost two-thirds of the present state of Ohio and parts of Indiana, West Virginia and Pennsylvania.

William McMechen, who had nine children to two wives Rachel Rosanna Nivens (she died in 1751) and Sidney Johnson, was elected a member of the Continental Congress and when he died in 1797 aged 73 he left a large and prosperous estate.

Dr James McMechen, a year younger than William, married Agnes Carson, who inherited large tracts of land at White Clay Creek on the death of her father, and, while James moved west with his brother to Marshall county, West Virginia and survived numerous Indian attacks, he did not remain there.

James made his home at Berkeley Springs in what today is part of Morgan county, West Virginia and one of his closest associates in the region was James Rumsey, a man accredited by many as being the inventor of the steamboat a decade before second generation Ulsterman Robert Fulton, from Lancaster in Pennsylvania, came up with his theories on the application of steam to water navigation.

A business partnership in the construction of boats was forged in 1784 between James McMechen and James Rumsey and their work in maritime development enjoyed the patronage of General George Washington, who was keen to exploit the Potomac River for commercial purposes.

In 1785, the McMechen-Rumsey company opened a channel from Georgetown (Washington) to the Shenandoah Valley at what is now Harper's Ferry. The ties between the two men, however, loosened, when Rumsey went to Philadelphia and with the help of Benjamin Franklin and others to form the Rumsean Society to raise money for boats, not just in America but in England and France.

James McMechen had still continued his interest in steam-powered boats, but, on Rumsey's sudden death in London in 1792, he returned to his native Delaware to inherit land left by his brother David. He died in 1811.

Judge David McMechen, a son of William and Rachel Rosannah McMechen, did not accompany his father to West Virginia, but instead went to Baltimore, Maryland and became one of the richest men in that city. In 1780, he donated £500 to pay soldiers serving in the Revolutionary War and a year later was appointed a member of a committee to circulate new American paper money.

The Judge held strong anti-federalist views and he was a representative to the Maryland state legislature. Families belonging to the McMechen clan, some bearing names such as McMakin, McMichen, McMeekin, McMackin and McMicken, can be traced to frontier settlements at Rowan County, North Carolina; Spartanburg, South Carolina; East Tennessee and Kansas.

• A McMichen family from Ulster settled in Spartanburg, South Carolina in the late 18th century. One of the family John Hiram McMichen married a Jane Armstrong, who was born in Drung, Co. Cavan and emigrated with her parents and brother in 1825. From this family is descended Clayton McMichen, the celebrated American country music entertainer of the early part of this century.

5

Laying claim *to frontier land*

U pper Octorara lays claim to being the oldest Presbyterian church in the west Chester-east Lancaster county region of Pennsylvania and its first full-time pastor was Ballymena, Co Antrim-born the Rev Adam Boyd. The congregation was formed in 1720 by families who moved from the north of Ireland and Scotland a few years earlier and were first settlers in that part of the American frontier.

The first minister to preach at Upper Octorara (originally known as Sadsbury) was Welshman the Rev David Evans, who was also on pulpit supply on successive Sundays to nearby eastern Pennsylvania churches at Tredyffrin, Forks of Brandywine, Conestoga and Donegal.

David Evans held the pastorship for three years until 1723 when he moved to a church in New Jersey and for a year Scotsman the Rev Daniel Macgill was in charge. The ministry became more permanent when 32-year-old Adam Boyd arrived in September, 1724 with a certificate of his "good character" in America and preaching testimonials. For the next 44 years he was a popular occupant of the Upper Octorara pulpit.

Ten days after Adam Boyd's installation he married Jane Craighead, daughter of leading Presbyterian frontier cleric the Rev Thomas Craighead, and very soon his ministry extended over a vast territory of Eastern Pennsylvania, leading to the formation of congregations at Forks of Brandywine, Middle Octorara, Leacock, Pequea, Donegal, Doe Run, Coatesville, Belleview, Waynesburg, Penningtonville and Fagg's Manor (Londonderry township).

The first meeting house at Upper Octorara was a log cabin structure about thirty-five by forty feet square, in the tradition of 18th century Presbyterian churches. Adam Boyd is described as "a man of great exactness" who it was said kept a book full of minute memoranda until his last days.

At the time, ministers collected their own stipends and in his minuted account Boyd details the payments of each subscriber, whether in money, produce or otherwise, alongside the outgoings. The annual stipend during his ministry varied from £30 to £60, but his income was obviously augmented by donations from other congregations where he preached, from bequests and from money raised through his small land holding.

The Rev Adam Boyd left five sons and six daughters. John, the oldest, was licensed to preach, but died young; Thomas inherited the family lands along with Andrew, who was a militia colonel in the Revolutionary War; Adam founded the Cape Fear Mercury newspaper at Wilmington in North Carolina and as a Presbyterian minister was chaplain of the North Carolina brigade, while Samuel, the youngest, became a doctor.

Three of Adam Boyd's daughters married Presbyterian ministers. Adam Boyd's marriage-portions to his daughters were large, according to the traditions of the day: on the marriage of his eldest daughter, he gave her, besides a silk gown, a bed and its furniture, a horse and a saddle, and nearly every article for housekeeping, all of which was carefully entered in his book.

Cornelius Rowan and Arthur Park - the two men who represented the Upper Octorara congregation in making the call to Adam Boyd - were both Ulster-born and were among the earliest settlers in the region. Rowan was a man advanced in years and he died just a year after Adam Boyd's installation. In his will, he speaks of himself as "late of Ireland" and mentions his wife Ann "now in Ireland." He emigrated to America with his son Abraham and daughter Ann.

Arthur Park was a native of Ballylagby, Co Donegal and he arrived in America with his wife Mary and four children and other members of the wider family in 1720. Among the household articles Arthur and Mary Park brought with them was a pewter platter, about seventeen inches in diameter with the initials "A. M. P." stamped upon it. The platter remains in the possession of a Park (Parke) descendant, who is attached to the Octorara congregation.

Halfway through the Rev Adam Boyd's ministry at Upper Octorara there occurred "the great schism" in the American Presbyterian Church based mainly in Pennsylvania and Virginia and for 17 years until 1758 congregations divided over their interpretations of the "Great Revival" of 1740, which was inspired by the preaching of English evangelist the Rev George Whitefield.

Upon Whitefield's first arrival in America in 1739, the spirit of revival extended over a wide area, with the large throngs of people who flocked to hear him literally hanging on his every word. Historic accounts reveal that the worshippers "yielded themselves in large numbers to an excessively emotional conversion and were permanently transformed in character".

Over a period of 20 years, George Whitefield made a total of seven journeys to the American colonies and his influence on evangelical church life in embryonic states like Pennsylvania, Georgia and Virginia was considerable. His achievements included the formation of 150 Congregational churches on American soil; preparing the way for the establishment of the Methodist Church in America and the building of the Princeton and Dartmouth theological colleges.

Whitefield was chiefly the means of rejuvenating the Presbyterian, Episcopal and Baptist churches, and it was observed that even the Society of Friends or Quakers were awakened by his inspirational labours.

Supporters of the Whitefield ministry in America on the "New Side" of Presbyterianism regarded all who opposed them as being in opposition to the glorious work of Grace, and as enemies of God, and of being unconverted men and hypocrites. Those in opposition on the "Old Side" censured the "extravagant measures" employed in witnessing for the faith and they were also offended at what they deemed was the harsh and uncharitable spirit with which they were denounced.

The "Old Side" group strongly maintained the idea of "God's working in an orderly manner through constituted authority lodged in the hands of men educated and ordained in the orthodox tradition of the Scottish or Irish Presbyterian Churches, and sent forth in that authority on specific missions to preach the truth, producing a salvation evident primarily to God in its manifestations and never audible or visible to man in its emotional expression."

The "New Side" lobbyists promoted vigorously the idea that the genuine spiritual inner experience of God's grace must change human conduct to conform to the will of God and particularly so for the ministry. The evidence of this experience was to be controlled, but it was frequently audible and visible in its physical manifestations.

They held that the church presbytery had no right to exercise its authority contrary to these directions of the Spirit, especially concerning when and where a minister should preach. The right of "intrusion" became a bitter point of debate.

The schism was widened when the Synod of Philadelphia adopted a ruling preventing the admission of "uneducated men" into the ministry through the growth of itinerant preaching. During the controversy many Presbyterian ministers were accused of clinging to a "dead orthodoxy" and as the revivalist movement progressed it sharply brought into conflict the two ideas of entering the domain of salvation - by the traditional training methods and nurture or by cataclysmic conversion.

Adam Boyd and a minority of his congregation sided with the "Old Side", but a majority withdrew and organised a "Second" Upper Octorara church in 1741. The Rev Andrew Sterling, another Irish-born cleric, became "Second" pastor in 1747 and the leading families in this new church were the Hamills, Boggs, Cowans, Glendennings, Kyles, Sharps, Dickeys, Moodys, Wilsons, Kerrs, Summerills, Robbs, Hendersons, Sandfords and Allisons. The two meeting houses were about a mile distant from each other.

The early Scots-Irish Presbyterian settlers brought with them the traditional customs and modes of worship of their churches back in the homelands. One of these was that of having two consecutive services on the Sabbath, with an intermission of half an hour. This custom prevailed well into the 19th century and usually worshippers were refreshed at the nearby river spring and readily ate what was available in outdoor meals prepared by the womenfolk of the community.

Andrew Sterling, autocratic and impetuous in his ministry, also had charge of the Doe Run congregation, while Adam Boyd took on extra duties by ministering at the Forks of Brandywine church. The split in the wider Presbyterian church was healed in 1758, but First and Second Octorara congregations remained apart for another decade.

The Rev William Foster, who succeeded Boyd and Sterling, was born at Little Britain township in Lancaster county, Pennsylvania, the son of Alexander Foster, who emigrated from Co Londonderry. Foster, a man of great piety and common sense, was a unifying spirit in the region, having turned down two other calls to accept the ministry of Upper Octorara in 1768.

William Foster married Hannah Blair, daughter of the Rev Samuel Blair, a leading Presbyterian cleric of the time, and he led his people in the struggle for independence during the Revolutionary War. On one occasion Foster was called to Lancaster to preach to militia troops gathering before they joined up with the main revolutionary army and his sermon was "so acceptable" that it was printed and circulated to provide inspiration for the spirit of patriotism among the people.

This was in the pattern of Foster's clerical contemporaries and it motivated British army officers to go to great lengths to silence the Presbyterian men of the cloth. On one occasion, British forces, riled by Foster's radical views, attempted to take him prisoner and burn down the Upper Octorara church. But they were foiled by Foster's vigilance and the loyalty of his congregation who rallied in defence. Foster, worn out by his labours, died in 1780 aged only 40.

William Foster left a widow and four sons and four daughters, the eldest only 14 and the youngest a year. Two of the sons, Samuel Blair Foster and Alexander W. Foster, became members of the Bar and they were among the most eminent lawyers of western Pennsylvania.

William Foster was succeeded at Upper Octorara by the Rev Alexander Mitchel, who had a stormy eleven-year ministry which resulted in 1796 in him requesting the Presbytery to end the pastoral relationship. For the next 14 years, the Upper Octorara congregation managed without a full-time pastor and the reins were taken up in 1810 by the Rev James Latta, the son of an Irishman who went on to complete a 40-year highly productive ministry.

Man with a mission

The Rev John Cuthbertson - the first American missionary from the Reformed Presbyterian Church in Ireland - travelled an estimated 60,000 miles on horseback during his 39-year mission in the Appalachian territory.

North Antrim man Cuthbertson, recalled who enduring a rough 46-day sea journey in 1751 from "Derry Loch to New Castle, Delaware", was said to have preached on 2,400 days and baptised 1,800 children during his Covenanting ministerial career on the frontier.

His mission field stretched for hundreds of miles along the Great Wagon Road from Pennsylvania through the Shenandoah Valley to south western Virginia where the Scots-Irish families had moved and settled.

6

MacGregor's clan *from the Bann Valley*

The First Parish Church at East Derry in New Hampshire was the first Presbyterian meeting house opened in New England, founded in 1719 by Presbyterians from Aghadowey, Coleraine and Macosquin in the Bann Valley area of Ulster. The Church is now listed in the American Register of Historic Places.

The original East Derry settlement was quite small with only about 20 families, but the population rapidly increased when more immigrants arrived in from Aghadowey and the surrounding Bann Valley hinterland. They had come on the recommendation of the Rev William Boyd, who, in the spring of 1718, arrived in Boston as their agent.

Aghadowey, a fertile region bordering on Co Antrim and Co Londonderry, was once described as "the Garden of Ulster" and its people "the salt of the earth". The area was settled by lowland Scottish Presbyterians as early as 1612, but most arrived after the 1641 rebellion by the native Irish Roman Catholic population and in the years before the 1680s-1690s Williamite Wars in Ireland.

It is recorded that the Presbyterian people of Aghadowey - weavers, bleachers and artisans - spoke as pure Scotch as one might hear in any part of Ayrshire or Argyllshire. They were a civilised and industrious people who kept their homes "cleanly and orderly".

Various reasons are given for the very early 18th century emigration to America by the Aghadowey Presbyterians. At the time, many unscrupulous landlords increased the rents, by double and even treble the amounts. There was also six years of drought in that part of Ulster between 1714 and 1719, but what most influenced this proud and determined people was the persecution they faced from the established Episcopal Church through the terms of the 1703 Test Act.

Presbyterian clergymen were not recognised by the law, with marriages and baptisms performed by them not considered legal. It therefore galled the Presbyterians that Roman Catholic priests, who were regarded as "enemies", did have formal authority on the administering of their church doctrine and practice.

The Presbyterians also deeply resented having to pay tithes for the upkeep of an Episcopal church system (Anglican or Church of Ireland) they did not belong to and which had no sympathy for them.

The Rev James MacGregor, who led the Bann Valley Presbyterians to America, was the third minister of Aghadowey and the first to be born in Ulster. He was the son of Captain MacGregor, of Magilligan, and as a youth he was in Londonderry during the Siege of 1688-89 and was said to have fired the gun announcing the approach of the 'Relief' ships up the Foyle

MacGregor was educated at Glasgow, ordained in Aghadowey in 1701 and he married Marion Cargill, daughter of David Cargill, a ruling elder in the church. Because the lands in the Aghadowey township were Episcopal church-owned or in the hands of London-based business interests, the Aghadowey congregation experienced great difficulty in obtaining a farm and maintenance for their minister.

Interesting data contained in the Aghadowey Presbyterian session book from 1702 shows a number of cases coming before the elders involving marriages of congregation members carried out by the local Roman Catholic priest.

A reason for this could have been lack of parental consent, but it may very probably have been attributed to the fact that Presbyterian ministers were not legally permitted to officiate at weddings and the choice of the priest over the Episcopal rector may have been considered by some families as the lesser of two evils. It meant a great deal to parents of the period to have their children legally married.

The MacGregor party (reliable estimates 600) from the Bann Valley arrived in five ships at Boston harbour on August 4, 1718. They were immigrants recruited from an area covering a 25-mile radius which included Aghadowey, Macosquin, Coleraine, Kilrea, Garvagh and

Ballymoney. MacGregor's brothers-in-law James McKeen and James Gregg, both of whom were married to Cargill girls, had a leading role in the movement.

MacGregor's text on his eve-of-departure sermon in Aghadowey Presbyterian Church was: "If Thy presence go not with me, carry us not up hence."

The Bann Valley Presbyterians introduced two commodities into New England that had never before been seen there - the small flax spinning wheel and the Irish potato, which was different from the American-grown sweet potato, but was looked upon as good staple food by the Ulster folk and complemented by the nutritious bean porridge and barley broth they brewed from the healthy land ingredients of the New World.

The Ulster-Scots were well versed in supplanting cottage industry and the means of providing very necessary food supplies.

In April, 1719, sixteen Presbyterian families from the Bann Valley in Ulster settled in two rows of cabins along West Running Brook to the east of Beaver Brook. Initially known at Nutfield, the New Hampshire settlement became Londonderry in 1723. In the first year, a field was planted known as the Common Field, where the potato was first grown in North America.

The first Londonderry log house was built for the Rev John MacGregor, but such was the danger of Indian attack that two strong stone garrison forts had to be quickly erected. Despite the precarious situation, however, Londonderry emerged through the middle part of the 18th century as a settled community and ten neighbouring New Hampshire townships were developed by offspring of the families, as well as two in Vermont and two at Nova Scotia in Canada.

Fifty of the intake of Scots-Irish families from the Bann Valley were initially settled in the New England colonial township of Worcester where fifty log houses were erected. Later in 1739, the town of Coleraine, 50 miles from Worcester, was settled by members of these families.

The Worcester Scots-Irish petitioned to be released from paying money to support the Anglican form of worship, as they desired to support their own Presbyterian mode of faith. Their application was rejected and for several decades they bore the brunt of discriminatory practices by the ruling Episcopal classes, and even damage to their church property by hostile interests.

Warren in Maine was settled in 1735 by 27 Scots-Irish families, some of whom had come to Boston with the first wave in 1718 and others were of later emigration.

The Scots-Irish families at Salem in Washington county, New York, came from Monaghan and Ballybay in Ulster under the guidance of their minister the Rev Dr Thomas Clark. The Clark group sailed from Newry on May 10, 1764 and in September, 1765 he obtained twelve thousand acres of land to settle his families. A few families headed to the South Carolina up-country, but by 1767 most were installed at Stillwater (later called Salem) on individual tracts of 28 acres.

Dr Clark, a Scotsman, was minister of Ballybay (Cahans) Presbyterian Church from 1751 to 1764 and he was recognised as an itinerant preacher in Counties Monaghan, Tyrone, Down and Armagh. One of his congregation, John Hearst, was the forebear of the family who set up the wealthy Hearst publishing dynasty in the United States in the 19th century. He and his wife, Elizabeth Knox, emigrated in the 1764 voyage for a fare of four shillings and eightpence each and they settled at Long Cane close to Abbeville in the South Carolina up-country.

Later immigrants, encouraged by the Clark movement, were enlisted from Presbyterian congregations in Monaghan, Castleblayney, Clones, Cootehill, Ballybay, Caledon, Armagh, Dungannon and Stewartstown. Their ports of entry were New York and New Castle (Delaware)

7

Scots-Irish tradition *of church and school*

Presbyterian concern for education manifested itself in a big way in the 18th century frontier regions of Virginia, North Carolina, South Carolina, Tennessee, and Kentucky, just as it did earlier in the eastern seaboard states which were a landing point for the immigrants from Ulster and Scotland.

From they first arrived in America at the turn of the 17th-18th centuries, the Scots-Irish immigrants set about establishing a church, and alongside it a school, and this extremely important Calvinist ethos pertained for the next century and a half right across an expanding nation.

The Presbyterian tradition of church and school dates back to the teachings of Scottish reformer John Knox, who in his First Book of Discipline in 1560 instructed that "everie severall churche have a school maister", and that each father in a congregation be compelled, no matter what his "estair or conditioun", to bring up his children in "learnying and virtue".

Renowned Anglican bishop Gilbert Burnet while on a tour of Scotland in the late 17th century was much impressed by the Presbyterian regard for education. He was surprised to find even "a poor communality" able to dispute fine points of secular and sacred government and was even more surprised to find knowledge "among the lowest of them, their cottagers and servants." So it was in Scotland, in Ulster, and in America where the Presbyterians settled.

The Presbyterian community who moved from the Bann Valley in Ulster to New Hampshire in 1718 had a meeting house erected within a year of their arrival and, within six years, had established four schools in their Londonderry township.

In 1785 the Presbyterian Synod of New York and Philadelphia set down a marker that underlined official Scots-Irish thinking on this key aspect of church-school life: "That all our congregations to pay a special regard to the good education of children as being intimately connected with the interests of morality and religion; and that . . . the session, corporation, or committee of every congregation, be required to endeavour to establish one or more schools . . . and endeavour to induce the people to support them by contributions . . . that the Presbyteries appoint particular members or committees to visit the school, or schools, at least once in three months, to inquire into the conduct of the master, and the improvement of the children . . . that the Presbyteries, in appointing ministers to supply vacant congregations, require it as an indispensable part of their duty, to visit at the same time the schools, and require at the next meeting of the Presbytery, an account of their fidelity in this respect, and of the state of the schools, and that, in these schools effectual provision be made for the education of the children of the poor."

The early schools on the American frontier generally took the name of academies, with the characteristic features semi-public control and a broadened curriculum from primary to secondary level.

They were modelled on the first academy in Philadelphia, founded by Benjamin Franklin in 1751, with the teaching of humanities and classical learning the cornerstone. Some academies gave equal opportunities to girls along with the boys and this led to female higher education colleges.

School buildings in the early pioneering years were simple log cabins, but later some were of brick and stone. School equipment was extremely limited, with blackboards, maps, a few globes and some basic "philosophical apparatus" taking up some of the little space in the single classroom.

A few of the schools had small libraries of classical and English literature of the period and the educational horizons of the pupils were widened by the few books they could borrow from their teachers.

Discipline in the classroom was very rigid, the drill hard and the instruction from teachers remarkably thorough.

Many of the academies were under the control of Presbyterian congregations and their ministers, who in addition to their gospel calling, had an intense love of learning. President Andrew Jackson had a Presbyterian school education until he was 16 in the Waxhaws region of the Carolinas in the 1770s and early 1780s.

Presbyterianism was introduced in the American colonies in the latter part of the 17th century, with the first congregations set up in New England, New Jersey and Pennsylvania. Donegal pastor from the Irish Presbytery of Laggan the Rev Francis Makemie was in the vanguard of the early American church and his itinerant ministry and organisational abilities earned him the reputation of being "the father of American Presbyterianism".

Makemie, educated at Glasgow University, was a scholarly man who wrote a catechism in defence of the Calvinistic doctrines and the Westminster Standards of the church. He was a strong advocate of religious freedom in America and in 1707 he was imprisoned for six weeks by Lord Cornbury, the Anglican governor of New York, for preaching without a civil licence.

Francis Makemie was moderator of the first American presbytery formed in 1706. Its purpose, according to Makemie, was "to meet yearly, and oftener if necessary, to consult the most proper measures for advancing religion and propagating religion in our various stations, and to maintain such a correspondence as many conduce to the improvement of our ministerial abilities."

The firm foundations laid by Makemie allowed Presbyterianism to establish itself as arguably the most influential denomination in America in the 18th century. By 1740, the Church had established 95 congregations in the colonies, and, by 1780 when the United States was a fledgling nation, the number in the Appalachian states had reached 500.

The Rev Francis Allison, like Makemie a native of Co Donegal and a graduate of Glasgow University, was an educator who championed the twin-track church and school ethos in the American colonies and on the frontier. He emigrated to Pennsylvania in 1735 and, from 1737, pastored at the Presbyterian church in New London, and eight years on founded an academy there.

Allison had often lamented the absence of a school for the education of ministerial candidates and his teaching prowess was recognised when he later became rector of the Academy of Philadelphia.

Benjamin Franklin, a fellow Philadelphian, once described Allison as "a person of great ingenuity and learning, a catholic divine, and what is more, an honest man." Interestingly, Francis Allison was an "Old Light" Presbyterian who stood by the traditional Westminster Standards for the church.

Allison took a dim view of the Rev William Tennent's Log College of theology and other revivalist projects aimed at increasing the number of "New Light" ministers for congregations sprouting up along the frontier. With conciliatory sermons, however, Allison greatly influence a re-uniting of the two sides in 1758.

The Rev William Tennent was an ordained priest in the Church of Ireland, but when he emigrated from Co Armagh to Philadelphia in 1718 he acknowledged his misgivings about the Episcopal doctrine and asked the synod of Philadelphia to admit him to the Presbyterian Church.

The synod, after deliberating on Tennent's past ordination in Ireland, approved his request, but not before giving him a serious exhortation to "continue steadfast in his new holy profession".

For close on 30 years, William Tennent had a remarkable career as a Presbyterian minister and educator, singularly possessed with the aim of teaching young men the rudiments of evangelical theology and piety. He ministered in New York and Philadelphia, but pastored for twenty years until his death at Neshaminy church in Pennsylvania.

In 1735, he erected his Log College, an eighteen-by-twenty-foot wooden structure that is generally accepted as the precursor to the College of New Jersey (now Princeton - established 1746). Tennent's four sons - Gilbert, John, Charles and William Jun. - were among his Log College theological students, as were renowned 18th century frontier preachers the Revs Samuel and John Blair and Samuel Finley. Visits to the American colonies by English Methodist evangelist the Rev George Whitefield helped sustain William Tennent's brand of Calvinism and close links were also developed with the Dutch Reformed Church.

After a sojourn at the Tennent school in 1739, George Whitefield wrote: "The place wherein the young men study now is in contempt called The College. It is a log-house, about twenty feet long and near as many broad, and to me it seemed to resemble the schools of the old Prophets."

George Whitefield also spoke highly of the "searching" sermons of Armagh-born the Rev Gilbert Tennent, the first graduate of his father's Log college and who set about his largely itinerant ministry with fiery passion and zeal. In 1740, Gilbert Tennent caused controversy with a sermon "The Danger of an Unconverted Ministry" which held up to ridicule "orthodox, but impious ministers" who, according to Tennent, had "the form of religion, but no substance in faith".

Tennent's outbursts greatly contributed to the Old Side-New Side schism within American Presbyterianism in the 1740s, but when he moved to Philadelphia to pastor Second Presbyterian Church he became more accommodating to the views of other clerics and was elevated to the moderatorship of the New York-Philadelphia synod.

Pressure in the late 18th century for free schools, according to American historian Charles William Dabney, came from "the small farmers of the mountain, piedmont and hilly country" who had few or no slaves and who found it necessary to co-operate with their neighbours in educating their children.

These people were composed largely of Scots-Irish Presbyterians, German Lutherans and Moravians and French Huguenots.

Opposition to free schools supported by public taxation came from the wealthy slaveholding planters of the Tidewater and Piedmont regions of the older American states. This so-called aristocracy held to the English Anglican tradition that education was primarily for the privileged classes - the offspring of well-to-do "gentlemen" and those of the professional ranks who could afford to pay for it.

The one-room log cabin schools founded by the diligent Presbyterian pastors in time became academies and colleges. Some even progressed to university status, such as Liberty Hall Academy in Lexington, Virginia to Washington and Lee University; Blount College to University of Tennessee and Cumberland College to University of Nashville. The University of Georgia, University of North Carolina, Transylvania University in Lexington, Kentucky and the College of South Carolina were also cradled from a Presbyterian ethos.

At least twelve of these Presbyterian colleges were founded in the frontier back-country by 1750, and by 1770 more than thirty were operating. When the American Civil War started in 1861, there were 66 higher education colleges in the southern states, most of them church-controlled. Presbyterians ran seventeen colleges, Baptists eleven, Methodist nine, other denominations sixteen and thirteen with state or municipal patronage.

The progression of Presbyterian log cabin college to university status was rapid in Tennessee. The Rev Samuel Carrick moved from Virginia to organise two churches in the Knoxville area - Lebanon on the Fork and First Knoxville in 1791-92 - and he founded a school which the territorial legislature chartered as Blount College in 1794.

In 1806, the United States Congress, when adjusting the land claims of Tennessee, granted the state 100,000 acres for the establishment of two universities. The Congressional grant was divided between Carrick's Blount College at Knoxville and Cumberland College, another Presbyterian institution founded at Nashville by the Rev Thomas B. Craighead, who in 1785 established the first Presbyterian church in Middle Tennessee at Fort Haysboro.

Both colleges remained semi-state institutions for many years with Presbyterian affiliations. The name of Blount College was changed to East Tennessee College in 1807, then East Tennessee University in 1840 and University of Tennessee in 1879. Cumberland College became the University of Nashville in 1825.

Presbyterians on the American frontier were intensely proud of their church system of education which prepared young men for the ministry. They with some substance frequently forwarded the claim that "the most ignorant College learnt man could open the true meaning of the Scriptures better than the best and wisest of God's children that had not College education."

Princeton was conceived after William Tennent's death as an integrated institution, attracting inter-colonial and Protestant inter-denominational students. Scotsman John Witherspoon, who took over as principal in 1768, cultivated an ethos which he intended to sustain a Christian republic in the post-Revolutionary War period. Witherspoon was the only cleric to sign the Declaration of Independence and no single religious group was more firmly identified with the American revolutionary cause than the Presbyterians.

Not all Presbyterians, however, were totally sold on the idea on political independence from Britain, even considering the legacy of animosity between the Church of England and Presbyterianism. Some conservatives, many of them upper-class merchants in the established eastern seaboard areas of the American colonies, feared for the economic and security consequences in a withdrawal from the British Empire.

On the other hand, the Presbyterian radicals, consisting of "middle sort" frontier stock and working-class urban folk, furthered the revolutionary ideals by substantiating claims of discriminatory British policies against their interests over many years and sought to negate the influence of the ruling colonial classes.

In Pennsylvania, this group, against the backdrop of political agitation by academics like John Witherspoon, succeeded in wresting power from the Quaker ruling class who had been in power in Philadelphia from William Penn first settled the region at the beginning of the 18th century.

It is not an overstatement to suggest that John Witherspoon and his academic friends played a dominant role in the shaping of the intellectual culture of the new American nation. His Scots-Irish contemporaries included Maghera, Co Londonderry-born Charles Thomson, a Presbyterian elder who was to serve as secretary of the Continental Congress; John Livingston, a New York publisher, and Joseph Clark and James Armstrong, clerics who were to became moderators of the American Presbyterian General Assembly and militia officers.

In 1776, loyalist churchman the Rev Dr Charles Inglis, rector of Trinity Church in New York, noted with a degree of apprehension: " I do not know one Presbyterian minister, nor have I been able, after strict inquiry, to hear of any who did not by preaching and every effort in their power promote all the measures of the Continental Congress, however extravagant."

Throughout the War, Presbyterian clergy harnessed the opinion of their people in the drive for faith and freedom and, when the first General Assembly of the Presbyterian Church in the United States of America was established in May, 1789, the church was in a healthy condition.

In 1798 when some Irish Presbyterian radicals were agitating in support of the United Irishmen cause, the Presbyterian General Assembly in the United States circulated a pastoral letter warning of revolutionary democracy. The letter ran: "When formidable innovations and convulsions in Europe threatened destruction to morals and religion, when scenes of devastation and bloodshed, unexampled in the history of modern nations, have convulsed the word, and when our own country is threatened with similar calamities, insensibility in us would be stupidity; silence would be criminal. The watchmen on Zion's walls are bound by their commission, to sound a great alarm at the approach of danger."

The American Presbyterian General Assembly was divided among four synods - New York-New Jersey, Philadelphia, Virginia and the Carolinas, with 16 presbyteries, 177 ministers, 111 ministerial probations and 419 congregations. By 1800, the Presbyterian Ulstermen constituted the single largest non-English element of the white American population and their influence in the political direction of the nation was considerable.

Augusta Academy, the forerunner of the Washington and Lee University University at Lexington in the Shenandoah Valley, was the earliest educational institution west of the Blue Ridge Mountain in Virginia. It was founded in 1749 by Ulster-Scot Robert Alexander, a member of the Presbyterian Church at Timber Ridge, and when the Hanover Presbytery took control in 1776 the name was changed to Liberty Hall in accord with the patriotic sentiments of the time.

The one and a half storey log building in which the school began measured twenty-eight by twenty-four feet, but even through the difficult years of the Revolutionary War the rector the Rev William Graham managed in very basic conditions to turn out quite a number of students for leading public positions.

William Graham was described as "a most indefatigable and successful teacher of youth" and one of his brightest pupils was Isaac Anderson, whose grandparents on both sides of his family emigrated from Co Down in the early 1700s. Anderson entered Liberty Hall as a 15-year-old student and he graduated to become the minister of Washington Presbyterian Church about 10 miles from Knoxville.

Graduating under the Graham tuition were Scots-Irish pioneering Tennessee pastors and educators the Rev Samuel Doak (president of

Washington College and later founder of Tusculum College at Greeneville), the Rev Samuel Carrick (Blount College/University of Tennessee) and James Priestley (of Cumberland University, Nashville); eminent scholars and theologians such as Moses Hoge, George A. Baxter, Archibald Alexander, William McPheeters, John Holt Rice and Conrad Speece, as well as many lawyers and legislators who served the Commonwealth of Virginia and were instrumental in setting up the new states of Kentucky and Tennessee.

After the Revolutionary War, the Rev William Graham, supported by the Liberty Hall trustees and the Presbyterian synod of Virginia, formed a class of eight students for systematic training in theology. This class was significant in that it was the first theological school in connection with a college anywhere in America.

In 1798, President George Washington granted Liberty Hall 50,000 dollars, the largest grant up to that time in the history of American education, and the college, by then a university, was re-named in his honour. Confederate general Robert E. Lee was president of the university after the Civil War and he established many academic and social traditions which exist to this day. Lee's name was added to the title in 1871 to perpetuate his memory.

Dr Henry Ruffner, an early teacher at Liberty Hall, penned these highly colourful impressions of the College: "The schoolhouse was a log cabin. A fine forest of oaks, which had given Timber Ridge its name, cast a shadow over it in the summer and afforded convenient fuel in the winter. A spring of pure water gushed from the rocks near the schoolhouse. From amidst the trees the student had a fine view of the country below, and of the neighbouring Blue Ridge Mountains. In short, all the features of the place made it a fit habitation of the woodland muse, and the hill deserved its name of Mount Pleasant.

"Hither about thirty youth of the mountains repaired, 'to taste of the Pierian spring', thirty-five years after the first settlement of Burden's Grant. Of reading, writing and ciphering the boys of the country had before acquired such knowledge as primary schools could afford; but with a few exceptions, Latin, Greek, algebra, geometry, and such like mysteries, were things of which they knew perhaps to lie covered up in the learned heads of their pastors - but of the nature and uses of which they had no conception whatever.

" It was a log hut of one apartment. The students carried out their dinner with them from the boarding houses in the neighbourhood. They had their lessons either in the school-room, where the recitations were heard, or under the shades of the forest where breezes whispered and birds sang without disturbing their studies.

"A horn - perhaps a cow's horn - summoned the school from play, and the scattered classes to recitation. Instead of broadcloth coats, the students generally wore a far more graceful garment - the hunting shirt, homespun, homewoven and homemade, by the industrious wives and daughters of the land.

"Their amusements were not the less remote from the modern tastes of students - cards, backgammon, flutes, fiddles and even marbles were scarcely known among these homebred country boys. Firing pistols and ranging the fields with shotguns to kill little birds for sport they would have considered a waste of time.

"As to frequenting tippling shops of any denomination, this was impossible because no such catchpenny lures for students existed, or would have been tolerated. Had any huckster of liquors, knicknacks, and explosive crackers hung out his sign in those days, the old puritan morality of the land was yet vigorous enough to abate the nuisance.

"The sports of the students were greatly gymnastic, both manly and healthful, such as leaping, running, wrestling, pitching quoits, and playing ball. In the rustic scenery a considerable number of boys began their education, who afterwards bore a distinguished part in the civil and ecclesiastical affairs of the country."

During the American Civil War of 1861-64, faculty and students of Liberty Hall (Washington Lee) carried on the radical tradition inherited from the Revolutionary War period, and their action in flying the Confederate flag over the campus led to the resignation of the College principal for twelve years, the Rev Dr George Junkin.

Dr Junkin, whose family had moved from Ulster to America in the 18th century, had two sons-in-law as principal officers in the Confederate Army - General Thomas Jonathan 'Stonewall' Jackson, married to Eleanor Junkin, and Colonel William Preston, married to Margaret Junkin. However, this did not prevent Dr Junkin objecting strongly to the flying of the Confederate flag at the College and at sentiments expressed by faculty colleagues in favour of Virginia's secession from the Union.

"The right of secession is a natural wrong. It is the essence of all morality. It neutralises the highest obligations," said Dr Junkin, on resigning his position in April, 1861. His stand came after members of the Virginia legislature proclaimed their oath null and void and said they had no allegiance to the United States of America.

Junkin was accused by his detractors of being a "Pennsylvanian Abolitionist" and called "Lincoln Junkin". His protestations came to naught; the Confederate flag remained on top of the College for almost the entire duration of the War.

Despite his views on the War and the prediction that the South faced disaster from the hostilities, Dr. Junkin never forgot his students and after the bloodbath of Gettysburg in 1863 he went to the battlefield to seek out Confederate prisoners. At the hospital he met a number of his Washington College students and preached to them.

Most were glad to see him and as they gathered around him, he took from his pocket the old class-book and commenced to call the roll and rehearsed the history of each student. He showed how all had suffered in consequence of their resistance of what he described as "the best government God had ever given to man".

George Junkin died in 1868 and was buried in Pennsylvania. Years later when the bitterness of the Civil War was reduced, his remains were brought back to Rockbridge county in his beloved Shenandoah Valley and interred in Lexington cemetery next to the grave of his illustrious son-in-law, General Thomas Jonathan "Stonewall" Jackson, a soldier with family roots in the Birches area of Co Armagh.

In the Matter of Rest

Rest for hand and brow and breast,
For fingers, heart and brain;
Rest and peace! along release,
From labour and from pain;
Pain of doubt, fatigue, despair ,
Pain of darkness everywhere,
And seeking light in vain.

Peace and rest! Are they the best,
For mortals here below?
Is soft repose from work and woes,
A bliss for men to know?
Bliss of time is bliss of toil:
No bliss but this, from sun and spoil,
Does God permit to grow.

• A description of blissful toil by pioneering settlers in the Blue Ridge Mountains - by Judge Logan E. Bleckley, of Rabun county, Georgia. Judge Bleckley was of Scots-Irish stock.

8

Pioneers of education
in the Great Smoky Mountains

Maryville College - the third oldest educational institution in Tennessee - was established on the initiative of the Rev Dr Isaac Anderson, the grandson of a Co Down Presbyterian and a descendant of family members who fought at the Siege of Londonderry in 1688-89.

In 1818, Dr Anderson, pastor of New Providence Presbyterian Church at Maryville in the heart of the Great Smoky Mountain region, expressed concern at the serious scarcity of ministers in the Tennessee-Kentucky-Virginia-North Carolina frontier region and he appealed to church leaders in the New England region to persuade at least six young men to take up the challenge.

Initially, only one heeded the call - a 16-year-old bootmaker's apprentice Eli Sawtell, who with fortitude walked for seven weeks through rugged dangerous terrain to reach the Maryville destination, a distance of 1100 miles.

Eli Sawtell's meagre belongings included a small Bible, Isaac Watt's hymnbook, a hickory walking stick and 14.60 dollars in money and it was said that "like Job's messenger in the Bible", he alone was left to bear tidings to Isaac Anderson. Maryville at the time was a small township with about 50 houses and 250 inhabitants and, for Eli, the log home and New Providence Presbyterian Church were not difficult to find.

Isaac Anderson, with support from the Rev James Gallagher, pastor of Rogersville Presbyterian Church, founded Maryville College in

1819 as a theological institution offering a three-year curriculum which included courses on Hebrew Bible, Greek New Testament and the composition and delivery of sermons.

The first ministerial graduates were Eli Sawtell (the initial recruit), Elijah M. Eagleton, William A. McCampbell, William Minnis and Hilary Patrick. Their eligibility as pastors was determined by their declaration of "hearty approbation of the articles of the Confession of Faith and the Presbyterian mode of church government."

Eli Sawtell for some years after his graduation went about the country as an itinerant preacher raising money for the Maryville College. He also served for six years as minister of Washington Presbyterian Church and for a decade was chaplain to American seamen in Le Havre, France.

The Andersons were the descendants of Isaac and Martha Anderson and Samuel Shannon, heroes of the Siege of Londonderry in 1688-89. The Anderson and the Shannon families emigrated to America early in the 18th century and Samuel Shannon's daughter Mary married James McCampbell in the Shenandoah Valley of Virginia. Later, the McCampbells moved with the Anderson and the Smith family to Grassy Valley, ten miles north east of Knoxville where the Washington Presbyterian Church is located.

Isaac Anderson's father William was a farmer, herdsman and hunter and as a soldier he took part in various militia campaigns against the Indians. He was a man of strong Christian ideals and in the Anderson home morning and evening a hymn was sung, a passage of scripture read and a fervent prayer offered.

Mary Shannon McCampbell, Isaac Anderson's grandmother, taught him to read and write and she also told him stories about her parents' horrific experiences during the Siege of Londonderry. While living at Lexington in the Shenandoah Valley, Isaac attended the Liberty Hall Academy, later to become Washington and Lee University.

Isaac Anderson joined the church at 17 and within two years he was preparing for the ministry by studying with his pastor, the only means of theological education in the frontier backcountry areas without seminaries. His mentors were the Rev Dr Samuel Carrick, minister of First Knoxville Presbyterian Church and president of Blount College, which became the University of Tennessee, and the Rev Dr Gideon

Blackburn, whom he succeeded as pastor at New Providence Church in 1811.

At the time New Providence, with 209 members, was the largest Presbyterian church in the region and the Rev Isaac Anderson was promised a stipend of 400 dollars a year, a sum the congregation was not always able to meet. Anderson was more than a parish minister and teacher at Maryville College; he was a prolific writer of sermons and articles for church magazines, and also served as chaplain to a Tennessee militia brigade during the War of 1812.

He also supervised the erection of a road over the Great Smoky Mountains to Franklin in North Carolina. It was said that the Cherokees whom he supervised held him in such high esteem that "a letter of recommendation from Dr Anderson was the surest passport you could have to the confidence of the Cherokee tribes."

One of Dr Anderson's pupils was Sam Houston, a third generation Ulster-Scot who graduated to the status of teacher, politician, soldier and later governor of Tennessee and Texas. Sam's brother James was chairman of the Maryville College board in the 1820s.

Sam Houston's widowed mother Elizabeth, on the death of her husband Sam in 1807, brought her family of nine children from Lexington in Rockbridge county, Virginia to Blount County, Tennessee and they set up home at Baker's Creek close to the Little Tennessee River, about twelve miles from Maryville and on the border line between the white and Indian settlements. The Houston family, who had belonged to the Timber Ridge Presbyterian Church back in the Shenandoah Valley, joined the New Providence congregation.

Young Sam received practically all of his school training from Dr Anderson, who described him as "a young man of remarkably keen and close observation." Sam was 13 before he received any formal education, but he was a quick learner and soon had a firm grasp of the classics. By 18, he had graduated as a teacher.

Dr Anderson also said of Sam Houston: "Many times did I determine to give Sam Houston a whipping for neglect of study, but he would come into the classroom bowing and scraping, with as fine a dish of apologies as ever was placed before anybody, and withal so very polite and manly for one of his age, that it took all the whip out of me. I could not find it my heart to whip him."

When volunteers were called to fight the Creek Indians in the War of 1812-14, Sam Houston joined the army and he distinguished himself in the 7th United States Infantry at the Battle of the Bend of the Tallapoosa, where he received three wounds. He came to the attention of General Andrew Jackson - his rapid promotion as a soldier, and eventually as a politician had begun.

Other students at Maryville College were George Erskine, a former black slave who went to Africa as the first foreign missionary from the Union Presbytery in Tennessee, and John Gloucester, another black man who founded a church for blacks in Philadelphia. Cherokee and Choctaw Indians from mission churches in lower East Tennessee and North Georgia were among the early students at Maryville - further indication of Isaac Anderson's desire to include people of all races in his church and school.

Lack of finance contributed to slow progress in the first few years at the College, but the continued support of the New Providence congregation and generous donations, in cash and kind, from other churches and individuals kept the doors open. In 1824, New Providence Church donated the following for the upkeep of Maryville College: 252 bushels of corn, 452 lbs of pork, 331 lbs of bacon; nine bushels of sweet potatoes; 31 bushels of Irish potatoes; 21 bushels of turnips, 26 lbs of butter, 10 bushels of wheat, 26 loads of firewood, one barrel of flour. 18.27 dollars in cash, 12 pairs of socks, five yards of jeans, 20 yards of cotton shirting and one waistcoat.

The theological curriculum at Maryville was largely Biblical, with students being taught in their classes the Greek New Testament, the Hebrew Bible, Jewish Antiquities, Sacred Chronology, Biblical criticism, Metaphysics, Didactic and Polemic theology, church history and government, composition and delivery of sermons and duties of pastoral care.

By 1826, the number of Maryville students had grown to 40, with the Rev Isaac Anderson still the lone professor. Help came that year when the Rev William Eagleton was appointed as professor of sacred literature and he remained for three years.

His successor was the Rev Darius Hoyt, son of missionary to the Cherokees the Rev Ard Hoyt, and he assisted Dr Anderson as professor of languages. In 1831, the Rev Samuel McCracken joined them as professor of natural sciences, but left after a year to pursue a wider ministry and his place was taken by Kentuckian the Rev Fielding Pope, a professor of mathematics and natural philosophy.

Isaac Anderson continued as president of Maryville College until ill-health forced him to resign in 1855. The death in 1854 of his wife Flora McCampbell Anderson, whom he had married in the Shenandoah Valley in 1802, and a fire two years later which destroyed his home, along with his library, manuscripts, records and correspondence, were body blows to the old man. He died in 1857, aged 75.

Maryville College was by this time well established, although still inhibited in its progress through a lack of finance, and the new president was the Rev John J. Robinson. His tenure in office was interrupted by the turmoil of the impending Civil War and he left no one in any doubt about his Confederate sympathies, closing the college in 1861, "on account of a state of armed hostilities in the country."

Students and members of faculty went their way, some espousing the cause of the Union and others the Confederacy. The four teachers - three professors and a tutor - were equally divided - two for the Union and two for the Confederacy, a split which reflected the position in many communities at the time.

Interestingly, the Rev Isaac Anderson supported the abolition of the slavery movement and he vigorously opposed the idea of any state seceding from the Union. Under his presidency, the College was open to students of all races and colours and Dr Anderson's convictions were later espoused by Maryville academics Thomas J. Lamar and Gideon Crawford.

Of the 60 black students, attending Maryville College in the 35 years from the College's re-opening after the Civil War in 1866 to 1901 eighteen are known to have become teachers and 14 church ministers. In 1901 a Tennessee state law was passed forbidding black students to attend even white schools, but the US Supreme Court reversed this decision and Maryville College immediately resumed its policy of enrolling black students.

John J. Robinson departed for another school post at Rogersville, further into East Tennessee, and spent 13 years as a church pastor in Alabama.

While Maryville was not the site of major battles in the Civil War, its Great Smoky Mountain location made it vulnerable to army encampments and minor skirmishes. Both the Confederate and the Union armies in turn occupied the buildings of the College campus and it was from College Hill that General William Sherman sent his famous Union army message to General Ambrose Burnside in Knoxville: "Hold the fort for I am coming."

The College re-opened in 1867, under the leadership of Dr Thomas J. Lamar, a professor who had worked with Isaac Anderson, and when he stepped aside after a few years his place was taken by Dr Peter Mason Bartlett, who had ministered at New Providence Church.

One outstanding Maryville College professor who came from a similar Scots-Irish background to that of the Rev Isaac Anderson was the Rev Gideon Stebbins White Crawford, who spent 16 years tutoring at the College until his death in 1891, aged only 42. He was also superintendent for public instruction in Tennessee, a position now called Commissioner of Education.

Gideon Crawford's great grandparents, Andrew and Eleanor Crawford, were Co Antrim Presbyterian stock who came to America about 1750. They settled first in Pennsylvania, where a son Samuel was born in 1754. After the Revolutionary War, Andrew and his family moved to Rockbridge county in the Shenandoah Valley of Virginia and later proceeded to Hawkins county in North Carolina (today East Tennessee), living at Surgionsville near Kingsport.

Samuel Crawford, Gideon's grandfather, fought in the 1774 militia campaign against the Shawnee Indians and during the Revolutionary War he was attached to the Pennsylvania regiment. When he returned to Hawkins county, Samuel married Nancy Forgey, who had emigrated from Ulster with her parents Andrew and Peggy Reynolds Forgey, and in 1790 the couple moved to Grassy Valley near Knoxville and became involved with the Washington Presbyterian Church.

Family records confirm that Samuel Crawford "helped to raise the first log house where Knoxville now stands" - obviously a reference to the home of James White, the founder of Knoxville near the present site of the First Presbyterian Church. Samuel Crawford also joined his fellow frontiersmen in defending their homesteads from Indian attacks and on one occasion, in September, 1793, they repelled an attack on Knoxville by more than 1,000 Creek and Cherokee tribesmen.

Prominent in the defence of Knoxville from this attack was the Rev Samuel Carrick, from Lebanon in the Fork Presbyterian Church, who, although his wife had just died and was not yet buried, felt it was his duty to take his gun and to stand alongside the other men. Mrs Carrick was buried by the women of the church and, while the Knoxville defences held out, tragedy occurred at an isolated farmhouse a few miles from the town with the Indian massacre of 12 members of the Alexander Cavet family, who had surrendered after being promised that their lives would be spared.

Historian J. G. M. Ramsey, in his account of the incident, wrote that the Indians mutilated and abused "the bodies of the women and children especially, in the most barbarous and indelicate manner possible."

Samuel and Nancy Crawford had four sons and four daughters, and Hugh, Gideon's father, married Rebecca McPheters Crawford, whose direct Scots-Irish descendants Alexander and Mary McPheters were massacred by Indians in their home near Buffalo Gap in Augusta county, Virginia in 1764.

It was said that Hugh and Rebecca, who had twelve children, spoke with a "Celtic brogue", obviously inherited from their Scots-Irish family roots. Hugh Crawford was a ruling elder in Washington Presbyterian Church and the academic success of his son was a great pride to him and his wife.

Gideon Crawford was enrolled as a 17-year-old student at Maryville College in 1866 in what was to be the start of a link with the College which climaxed with a distinguished 17-year professorship from 1774 to 1791. Gideon, who taught mathematics and theological studies at Maryville, provided students and faculty with the inspiration and the resilience to establish the college as a main cornerstone for education in East Tennessee into the 20th century.

A fulsome tribute penned on his death stated: "Gideon Crawford was loyal to Presbyterianism in both its local and its general interest, but above all he was loyal to Christ. To Maryville College he gave his self-denying labors, his ardent prayers and his loving devotion."

* Maryville College is today a leading institution in the American educational sector, a college deeply embedded in Christianity, community and the liberal arts tradition. Of more than 2,000 similar-type colleges operating in the United States, Maryville College is

among the first fifty established, with several thousand students enrolled for the four-year courses from every state in the Union, and from various countries overseas.

The educational foresight and dedication shown by the Rev Isaac Anderson and his Scots-Irish contemporaries in the New Providence community of the early 19th century are perpetuated at this illustrious institution in the Smokies.

"Now faith is the substance of things hoped for, the evidence of things not seen." HEBREWS 11:1

Rev. Isaac Anderson (1782-1857), a beacon for Christianity on the American frontier.

9

Facing challenges *to their religion*

Scots-Irish Presbyterians, more than any other religious group, were firmly identified with the revolutionary cause in America and, as a denomination, they invested much of their identity in the war for independence.

It was British statesmen Horace Walpole who said in a jibe to his cabinet at the time of the revolutionary struggle: "I hear that our American cousin has run away with a Scots-Irish Presbyterian parson." His observation was hardly an over-statement, although up to a quarter of the Ulster Presbyterians remained loyal to the Crown.

The Rev John Witherspoon, leader of colonial Presbyterianism and founder of Princeton College in New Jersey, was the only minister to sign the Declaration of Independence in 1776. The Witherspoon commitment to constitutional change is summed up in a submission he made just before the signing of the Declaration: "There is not a single instance in history in which civil liberty was lost and religious liberty preserved entirely. If therefore we yield up our temporal property, we at the same time deliver the conscience into bondage."

Witherspoon's radical republicanism was shared by many other Presbyterian clerics. Some, however, were later to express much disillusionment at the outcome of the revolution, and its effects on the church as a driving force in government.

The ending of all compulsory public support for organised religion was a watershed in the new independence era which deeply divided the Presbyterians. Influential lay members of the church in Virginia believed that this was the right direction for the fledgling nation to go; others felt it was a retrograde step which allowed other Reformed denominations to supersede the Presbyterian witness in some areas.

The Methodists and the Baptists emerged in the later part of the 18th century as significant churches on the religious landscape of the south eastern states.

Whatever the competitions and new challenges they faced in late 18th century America, the Presbyterians remained a potent political, social and cultural force well into the 19th century. And, with their insistence upon college-educated clergy, they produced highly articulate and vocal clergy who made sure the interests of the church and their people were best served in the cities and towns where they ministered.

Legislation enacted from the War of Independence had the initial effect of making Presbyterian colleges more restricted in enrolment and more responsive to the promotion of church orthodoxy. But, by 1800, the Presbyterians were the single largest non-English sector of the white population in most Appalachian states and well into the century they held their position in American society, a confident people buoyed by the witness of their Calvinist beliefs and by the strength of their numbers.

Religion was an important ingredient in the lives of frontier people, back to the very first settlements. The church was the central core of the community in the early townships of Pennsylvania, Virginia, the Carolinas, Tennessee, Kentucky and Georgia and its influence impacted on the cultural and social life of the states. Presbyterian, Methodist and Baptist were the predominant faiths in the region and their teachings impacted on the generations who laid the foundations of a solid God-fearing society.

•••

• "By the time Tennessee became a state in 1796 Presbyterian congregations stretched from East Tennessee to Nashville. "John Calvin's spiritual descendants had become the state's most powerful religious force. And Presbyterians in those early days were associated so closely with education that they monopolised it."

Herman A. Norton, Religion in Tennessee

10

Living dangerously *on the Holston River*

The Reedy Creek settlement in the Holston River valley close to present-day Kingsport in north east Tennessee was pioneered in 1770-1773 by a group of Ulster families who had moved from the Shenandoah Valley in Virginia. This was one of the earliest encroachments by white families on to Tennessee land and their initial presence in dominant Indian territory was so minimal that the local Cherokee chief Attacullaculla uncharacteristically said that he "pitied them."

The white presence in this dangerous frontier region, however, was soon to be shored up by an influx of more Scots-Irish families from Virginia, their heavily-laden wagons climbing along the steep passes and the river valleys that lay between the Blue Ridge and the Cumberland mountain ranges.

The Holston region was first surveyed by two Englishmen James Needham and Gabriel Arthur about 1673 and for upwards of a century traders from Virginia followed the "Carolina Road" around the mountains to reach the "Overhill" Cherokee Indians.

The territory region was named after Stephen Holston, a south-western Virginia pioneer who in 1748 made a trip of exploration down the Holston, Tennessee, Ohio and Mississippi Rivers to reach the Natchez region. French explorers also moved through the region early in the 18th century and their rivalry with the English to raise first land stakes was intense and the representatives of both nations had their turns in currying favour with the Cherokee tribes.

The first Scots-Irish settlers at Reedy Creek were Humphrey Hogan, William Anderson, the Roberts brothers - Henry, John and David, John Clendenin, Archibald McNeal, Gilbert Christian and the McMillan, Williams and King families. Humphrey Hogan, a rugged long-hunter, is acknowledged as Tennessee's first schoolmaster, but his scholastic abilities were extremely limited as he could read but not write. Undeterred, he taught the children of Reedy Creek how to read and cipher. But their instinctive knowledge of hunting, fishing and managing to stay alive in the wooded, mountainous and river valley terrain was to stand them in good stead.

The area had been explored a year earlier by Captain Gilbert Christian, the son and grandson of Co Antrim Presbyterians who emigrated in 1732, settling in Lancaster county, Pennsylvania and then Virginia. Gilbert Christian later commanded the Sullivan county militia; fought at the Battle of Kings Mountain in 1780 and he enjoyed considerable repute as an Indian fighter. He built a cabin for his wife Margaret Anderson and five children seven miles up Reedy Creek.

Gilbert Christian commanded the King's Mill fort at Reedy Creek, but he was away from his post when the worst Indian atrocity of the period occurred on September 24, 1774. Chief Logan, a half-breed Mingo Indian from Ohio, and his tribesmen attacked the John Roberts family at their log cabin home, and massacred John, his wife and three children.

John's ten-year-old son James was taken prisoner and another younger son was scalped and left for dead. Within a week the injured boy - his skull cut open with a tomahawk - died from his injuries, lamenting in his last words that he "was not able to fight enough to save his mommy." His brother James was later returned home in a prisoner exchange.

The Roberts massacre caused great alarm to the neighbouring Reedy Creek families of Gilbert Christian, James Glendenin, William McNeal and William Anderson and they took temporary refuge in a deep sink hole at the top of a high ridge before reaching the safety of the heavily stockaded King's Mill fort.

John Anderson, the son of the early Reedy Creek settler William Anderson, colloquially detailed some of the customs of these early pioneer families: "The first settlers emigrated from nearly all states, but chiefly Virginia. Their manner and dress was generally pleasant and agreeable to themselves. Strict degree of temperance prevailed throughout this newly settled part of the country.

"At that time the dress of the men was hunting shirts and often leather britches and mockquesons and when they went abroad their hunting shirts were often neatly fringed with various colors and the sleaves neatly plaited.

"The women dress was commonly a short gown and other clothes plain and loose. No lacing was seen in that day. They appeared in a general way to enjoy fine health and great strength and many of them were beautiful. Their marriages were performed by Presbyterian ministers. Their fee was commonly that which was offered them.

"The people of that time appeared clean and neat in their houses. Their table was most frequently furnished with cornbread, meat, butter, and milk. There was no coffee or tea made use of in those days except of a domestic kind. There were few or no doctors as there was but little business for them and not sufficient to pay them for their attendance.

"There were no courts of justice in the country for some considerable length of time, but very few disputes and, of course, no law suits. They in general way appeared cheerful and happy when they were not disturbed by Indians."

Many of the first frontier settlers in South Western Virginia, East Tennessee and Kentucky were Revolutionary War soldiers who had received land grants and, invariably, for health reasons, they ensured that their homes were built near clear fresh water springs or streams. The homes were hewed log houses of rough red cedar wood, very often with no windows.

The early settler lived exclusively off the land, with enough bread made from the grain in the fields; meat from the animal herds and the wilderness; milk and butter from his cows; vegetables, melons and berries in the summer and, in winter, hickory nuts, walnuts, grapes, haws, persimmons. Sassafrass trees produced a root for tea and sugar maples provided sugar and syrup.

Cotton, flax and wool from the sheep were used in the clothing for adults and children, often manufactured without machines. The dye came from Indigo plants, saffron, walnut bark and roots and the madder plant. Corn and small grains and vegetables were grown for provisions for the family and the livestock.

Most late 18th century Scots-Irish frontier settlers were anti-federalist and their feelings of independence were summed by one North Carolinian, who mused:

"The country's a' in a greetin' mood,
An some are like to rin wud blud;
Some chaps whom freedom's spirit warms,
Are threatening hard to take up arms.
Their liberty they will maintain,
They fought for it, and they'll fight again."

Fall Creek on the north bank of the Holston River close to Reedy Creek was another first milestone in Tennessee where eighty-five Scots-Irish families ventured in the 1770-1774 period. They included Amos Eaton (one of the first to establish corn rights at Fall Creek!!), Moses and David Looney, Bryce Russell, Thomas Rainey, John Cox, John Coon, John Dever, David Erwin and John Patterson.

Other Scots-Irish staging posts in the region that developed apace were Sapling Grove (site of present-day Bristol); Watauga (Elizabethton); the Brown family settlement along the Nolichucky River; and Shoate's Ford (Bluff City).

A small Indian trading post was located at Long Island along the Holston River in 1770 by John Carter and William Parker. This twelve-mile square tract had been relinquished by the Cherokees, but in 1775 Shawnee Indians destroyed the trading post and the traders were forced to flee to the safety of the Watauga settlement.

Indian aggression in the Holston River settlements was effectively stemmed in July, 1776 when the Virginia Committee of Safety approved an all-out punitive expedition against the Cherokee tribes, led by Colonel William Christian. All the area forts housing the various families were defended by militia and scouts surveyed the countryside, and the Overhill towns of North Carolina, where the Indians lived, for signs of Indian attack.

Many of the older Indian chiefs wanted conciliation with the white settlers, but Dragging Canoe, the leader of the Cherokee war faction, was not for backing down. He was encouraged by two British agents Stuart and Cameron, working to an agenda that Indian attacks on the white settlements on the Holston River would considerably weaken the revolutionary forces in the war that had just begun.

The successful William Christian-led campaign against the Cherokees on the Little Tennessee River in the autumn of 1776 lasted four weeks and it led to the signing by militia leaders and Indian chiefs of the Long Island of Holston peace treaty of 1777. Violence still prevailed in this region through the war years with frequent Indian attacks on settler homes leading to more deaths, but the victory of the frontiersmen over British forces at the battle of Kings Mountain in October, 1780 stabilised settler life and, more content with their own security, they extended the frontier limits further into Tennessee with more confidence.

One significant Indian attack in the Holston River area was the massacre in November, 1777 at Carter's Creek of David Crockett and his wife, the grandparents of legendary frontiersman and politician Davy Crockett. The elderly couple were planting crops in the fields when Indians struck and brutally murdered them. One of their sons James was taken captive.

The divergent concepts of the Scots-Irish settlers and the Indian tribes of the Cherokees and the Shawnees are put into context by East Tennessee historians Carson and Alberta Brewer: "To a venturesome white settler searching for rich new land to plow, an Indian boundary meant little. Any land not cultivated, nor grazed by someone's cattle was his to take. To him, this was reasonable. But the Cherokees saw it differently. This land was theirs, though they built no rail fences around it. Not uncounted generations of experience, they knew much land was needed to provide all the deer, buffalo and other game without which their very existence would be jeopardised."

While Presbyterianism was the most dominant creed in the early Holston settlements of the 1770s-1780s, the Baptists and the Methodists were also a force to be reckoned with in the region.

Taylor's Meeting House, a Presbyterian establishment located in 1773 about four miles from the present-day town of Blountville, is claimed to be the first building erected in Tennessee for religious services. It is believed that all denominations worshipped there as the first settlements were too small for the organisation of one church. The first Baptist church in Tennessee was established at Buffalo Ridge,

Washington county in 1778, with a full Methodist circuit set up for the Holston region a few years later.

While the Presbyterian Church had a corps of highly educated evangelical ministers, their resources were greatly stretched over the vast terrain of frontier land and this resulted in some far-flung settlements being left to the ministrations of the Methodist circuit-riders and Baptist pastors, who were zealous in their propagation of the gospel with soul-stirring sermons.

Of the other religious denominations - Moravians, Lutherans, Episcopalians, Quakers and Roman Catholics, their numbers on this part of the frontier were very scarce and their influence minimal.

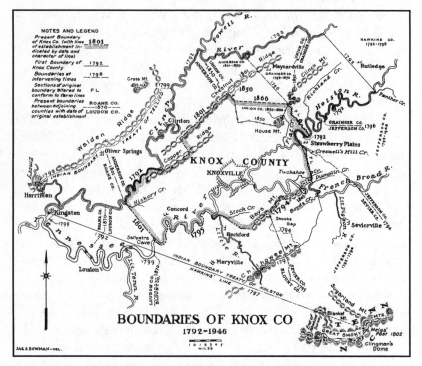

Early boundaries of Knox Country, Tennessee

11

Reverence towards God *on the frontier*

Eusebia - from the Greek word which means "reverence toward God" - was one of the first Scots-Irish Presbyterian settlements in East Tennessee, organised in 1786 by the Rev Archibald Scott from Virginia. Eusebia Church about 13 miles from Maryville in Blount county was erected on the site of the Great War and Trading Path, which had been home for several years to early settlers.

One of Archibald Scott's first duties was to give proper burial to womenfolk who died in the harsh frontier conditions. Scott's first sermon at Eusebia was preached under a large beech tree and the church was built near where the cemetery had been started. The Eusebia Presbyterian congregation really took root five years later when the Rev Gideon Blackburn arrived with a company of militia.

Gideon Blackburn, then only 20, was a graduate from the Rev Samuel Doak's Tusculum Academy at Greeneville, Tennessee. He was a tall impressive figure, not afraid to witness for the faith in any company, and although he intended to move on to new mission fields, his new flock, then numbering 40 families, implored him to stay, offering what was considered a reasonable stipend of 130 dollars a year as their permanent minister.

Gideon Blackburn remained at Eusebia for 15 years, preaching in the simple log cabin church in the clearing, to Scots-Irish families who had reached the Great Smoky Mountain region, from Pennsylvania and the Shenandoah Valley of Virginia: the McTeers, Bogles, Houstons, Pickens, McClungs, McAnallys, Creswells, McCroskeys, Malcolms, McCallies and McMurreys.

Robert McTeer's fort was close by the church and Gideon Blackburn ministered to his people, always with loaded musket at his side and a shot pouch over his shoulder in case hostile Indian raiding parties arrived.

It was said that Blackburn spent hours writing his sermons; he was a fire and brimstone preacher who did not mind extending his sermon beyond two hours. On one occasion, he spoke on a text for three and a half hours, and on another - at a funeral ceremony in the church graveyard - he kept 1,500 people in train to his Biblical discourse for several hours during a driving rainstorm.

Gideon Blackburn's sermons were often prepared as he worked at manual labour. When he ploughed he would have a piece of paper and an inkhorn on a stump at the end of a field. When he came to the end of a row, he would record on the paper the main headings of a sermon. While continuing to work in the fields, he would review the skeleton sermon, periodically stopping to write down the ideas that had come to him, until each part was filled out.

Blackburn left Eusebia in 1810 to take his message to the Cherokees Indians and he enjoyed relative success in this ministry with quite a number of conversions among the tribes. Christian schools were set up by Blackburn for the Cherokees and, in several tours of the South, he raised thousands of dollars for their upkeep.

The Cherokees, as a nation, worshipped a pagan god called the "Great Spirit" and confirmation of this emerged from discoveries among the contents of graves where, along with the dead, are deposited evidences of a belief in the immortality of the soul.

A dead pony or a broken bow were lain on the graves of departed warriors, testimony of the service the Cherokee tribes believed would be rendered in "the happy hunting ground" beyond the skies.

Cherokees, however, had no perception of heaven or hell or the hereafter, and all their invocations were made for temporal use and addressed to tangible gods. This is why Christian ministers on the frontier like the Rev Gideon Blackburn felt a pressing need to evangelise the Cherokee tribes to the truths of the gospel.

Frontier white settler views of the faith of the Indians tribes can best be summed up in the following lines: "Lo, the poor Indian, whose untutored mind, sees God in the cloud and hears Him in the wind."

The Presbyterian Church of America of 200 years ago saw itself as a missionary outreach for people of all races and in 1801 the Church's General Assembly called on its congregations to report on: 1, Indian tribes and methods used to reach them; 2, frontier settlements of interior parts of the country without religious instruction, and 3, the black population and methods best suited to their instruction.

During his time in Eusebia, the Rev Gideon Blackburn, whose main concerns were in the improvement of the economic conditions of the settlers and their spiritual welfare through the preaching of the gospel, helped in the establishment of churches in Knoxville and at Nashville (then Fort Nashborough).

The oldest gravestone in Eusebia cemetery is that of Joseph Bogle, who died in September 16, 1790. The Bogles had moved from the north of Ireland in the early 18th century. The cemetery is the site of Archibald Scott's old church campground. The present brick church at Eusebia was built in 1930 and the congregation still carries on the tradition of the first Scots-Irish settlers.

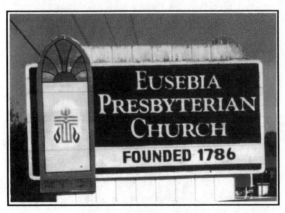

Sign for Eusebia Church.

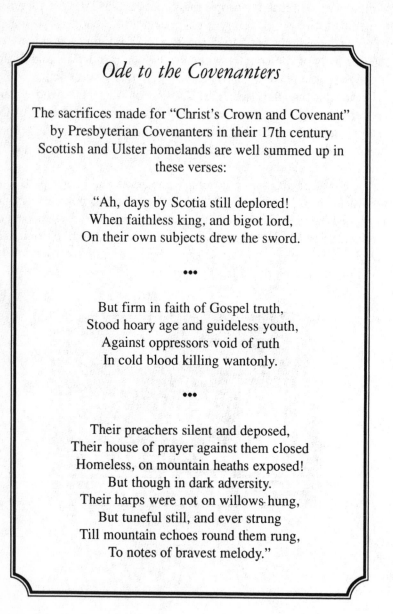

Ode to the Covenanters

The sacrifices made for "Christ's Crown and Covenant"
by Presbyterian Covenanters in their 17th century
Scottish and Ulster homelands are well summed up in
these verses:

"Ah, days by Scotia still deplored!
When faithless king, and bigot lord,
On their own subjects drew the sword.

•••

But firm in faith of Gospel truth,
Stood hoary age and guideless youth,
Against oppressors void of ruth
In cold blood killing wantonly.

•••

Their preachers silent and deposed,
Their house of prayer against them closed
Homeless, on mountain heaths exposed!
But though in dark adversity.
Their harps were not on willows hung,
But tuneful still, and ever strung
Till mountain echoes round them rung,
To notes of bravest melody."

12

Presbyterian outreach *in wild and desolate country*

The first Presbyterian church to be erected on Tennessee soil was in the Watauga Valley, the Holston river region which was originally part of North Carolina and for a few years comprised the lost state of Franklin. The Massengill House of Worship (or Meeting House) was established in July, 1777 under the supervision of the Rev Charles Cummings, but it was burned to the ground by Crown loyalists two years later in the communal bitterness surrounding the Revolutionary War.

Charles Cummings, a cleric ministering in the Abingdon area of south western Virginia, was the earliest Presbyterian minister to reach this outer frontier region and his arrival was hailed with great joy by the Scots-Irish settlers, who, it was reported at the time, were "hungering and thirsting for spiritual nourishment" in the wooded wilderness they were now occupying.

After preaching continuously for three days, the pioneering pastor organised the assembling of logs, boards and other materials required for the new meeting house in the clearing. Even church pastors had to put their hand to building and joinery in those days.

Cummings was in the mould of the frontier settlers he preached to: tough and direct, with a message that was fundamental to the spiritual needs of those who inhabited this wild and desolate countryside. Travelling through his parish on horseback, Cummings always had a long rifle at his side in case of Cherokee Indian attack. And when he preached, members of his congregation stood guard with long rifles in hand.

Notwithstanding the early arrival of Charles Cummings, a largely unknown Anglican pioneering preacher is remarkably believed to have been the first Protestant minister to set foot upon Tennessee soil. This was about 1760 when Tennessee was a wilderness, virtually uninhabited by white people.

The fall-out from events leading up to, during and following the Revolutionary War alienated the Episcopal Church from society in Tennessee for the next sixty years so uncompromising were the independent Scots-Irish Presbyterian settlers in their antipathy towards what they perceived as the established Church of England.

General George Washington, the hero of the American Revolution and most Scots-Irish settlers, may have been an adherent of the Episcopal faith, but this did not endear the dissenting Calvinists to his church, which they saw as being headed in London by the much despised King George 111.

The Scots-Irish settlers, clergy and laity alike, were fearless people; men and women who did not flinch before the terrors of the wilderness. On occasions, they were forced to shelter in forts for greater protection, but more often they were left alone on isolated farms to fend for themselves and their children. Survival on the frontier was entirely dependant upon quick wits and accurate marksmanship by the frontiersmen with their rifles.

Within a short period, Charles Cummings was joined at Watauga by the Rev Joseph Rhea, who for 20 years until 1769 had been minister of Fahan and Inch Presbyterian Churches in the Innishowen peninsula of Co Donegal. Rhea emigrated from the port of Londonderry with his wife and seven children and after ministering for four years at Piney Creek at Taneytown, Maryland, he turned his sights towards a fresh mission challenge in Tennessee.

Both men acted as chaplains to the local militia forces engaged under the command of Colonel William Christian in the 1776 campaign against the Cherokee Indians on the Little Tennessee River. Joseph Rhea was accompanied by his eldest son John in the Tennessee frontier mission and, after purchasing lands at Beaver Creek in 1777, he excitedly decided to return to Maryland to round up other members of the family for the trek westwards. Sadly, Rhea took ill suddenly with pneumonia and died in Maryland, aged 62. He did not manage to get back to Tennessee.

Joseph Rhea's wife Elizabeth, eldest son John and the rest of the family carried out his wish of removing to the Watauga region and after a hazardous six-week winter journey they reached their new home in the middle of a snowstorm in February, 1778.

The Rheas were followed to the Watauga region by other Ulster families from Donegal and Londonderry who were attached to the Piney Creek congregation, and, together, they formed in 1782 the New Bethel Presbyterian Church, situated a few miles from the site of the Massengill House of Worship or Meeting House close to present-day Kingsport.

The families who moved from Maryland included the Allisons, Andersons, Bredens, McCorkles, Lynns, McAllisters and the Hodges and their first minister at New Bethel was the Rev Samuel Doak, the son of a Co Antrim-born couple who had moved to the Shenandoah Valley from Pennsylvania in 1740, after surviving a severe winter in Ulster that became known as "the time of the black frost."

After the demise of the Massengill church, New Bethel became the oldest church in that part of Tennessee and its first ruling elders were James Gregg, Francis Harden and John Allison. Many of the first Scots-Irish settlers of the Holston region are buried in the New Bethel cemetery, including William and Isaac McKinley, family forebears from Co Antrim of President William McKinley.

From the earliest settlements, Kingsport was a stronghold of the Presbyterian Church, thanks to the firm foundations laid by pastors like Charles Cummings, Joseph Rhea and Samuel Doak.

Samuel Doak, an associate of the Rev Joseph Rhea, had been ministering in the Holston region since 1778 and owned a tract of 300 acres of land. He was pastor to the Concord and Hopewell congregations, and later to the Little Limestone community where the family of Davy Crockett settled.

Doak also acted as chaplain to the Scots-Irish militiamen who fought at the battles of Kings Mountain and Cowpens and, after several years spent in New Bethel, he founded Martin Academy at Salem, Washington county in 1783. The Academy later became Washington College in 1795 and when Samuel Doak retired in 1818 at the age of 69 he moved to Greeneville to establish the Tusculum classical school.

Martin Academy was chartered before any other educational institution west of the Allegheny mountains, with the Salem church and log schoolhouse sited on Samuel Doak's land. The site was extended by another 50 acres when Washington College came into being.

Samuel Doak was a Presbyterian pastor-teacher of the old school and he was easily identified by eccentric dress mannerisms that were uncommon to the American frontier: antique wig, old-fashioned shoes with broad shining buckles, long stockings and short breeches, ornamented with buckles on the knees.

President Theodore Roosevelt, in his book 'The Winning of the West', wrote of Samuel Doak: "Possessed of the vigorous energy that marks the true pioneer spirit, he determined to cast in his lot with the frontier folk. He walked through Maryland and Virginia driving before him an old 'flea-bitten grey' horse, loaded with a sackful of books; crossed the Alleghenies and came down the blazed trails to the Holston settlements.

"The hardy people among whom Samuel Doak took up his abode were to appreciate his learning and religion as much as they admired his adventurous and indomitable temper; and the stern, hard, God-fearing man became a powerful influence for good through the whole formative period of the South-West."

Roosevelt, in another of his clinical observations, pinpointed how the struggle for survival on the frontier was severe and off-times barbarous. "As the frontiersmen conquered and transformed the wilderness, so the wilderness in its turn created and preserved the type of man who overcame it. The influence of the wild country upon the man is almost as great as the effect of the man upon the country."

It was to these frontier people, conditioned and toughened by years of frontier life, that clerics like Samuel Doak brought the gospel message of Jesus Christ. As a strong Calvinist, Doak participated actively in the civil and political affairs of the country. He always voted, and, in the esteem he was held by his people, he was generally allowed to open the polls on election day, and vote first.

Samuel Doak always kept his rifle near at hand during services and on a number of occasions he is said to have stopped preaching and joined members of his congregation in pursuit of the Indians.

Churchmen were an integral part of the community - some operated without pay and made their living as farmers and hunters in the same manner as the other settlers.

When danger surfaced from Indian attack they were expected to take up arms in defence of the community. Samuel Doak was certainly in the mould of the preacher-frontiersman.

American cleric Bishop E. E. Hoss said of Doak: "He feared God so much that he feared nothing else and would have made a fit chaplain for Oliver Cromwell's Ironsides, a man of influence on the early history of the state of Tennessee."

Samuel Doak, in several journeys to eastern cities, assembled a library for Washington College which consisted of text books to be loaned out to the students in their literary course, and works of theology for students in divinity. The divinity students received their entire preparation for the ministry under the painstaking tuition of Doak. His first graduates at Washington College in 1798 were his own son John Whitefield Doak, and James Witherspoon.

The Rev John W. Doak was appointed financial agent for the College and in several tours to the south and east over a two-year period he reported an intake of $1,956, a sizeable amount of money for the period which was put to good use on the expanding Washington campus. John W. Doak succeeded his father as president of the College and with him as tutors were the Revs James McLin, Samuel Zetty and John V. Bovell. However, he died in 1820 and twenty years later another Doak, the Rev Archibald Alexander, became president.

Samuel Doak's Tusculum College outside Greeneville provided a practical education for about sixty students. There, Doak taught for twelve years until his death in 1830. Another son the Rev Samuel W. Doak took over as president in 1835 after the College had been closed for five years from his father's death and, from an initial four students, it rose again to sixty in 1840.

The College rapidly expanded through the latter part of the 19th century and, significantly, when a new building was erected in 1884 a 7,000-dollar donation was received from the estate of Cyrus Hall McCormick, the Shenandoah Valley (Virginia)-born inventor of the agricultural reaping machine. McCormick's 18th century Presbyterian ancestors emigrated to America from outside Dungannon in Co Tyrone.

Tusculum College was amalgamated in 1868 with Greeneville College, which was founded in 1796 by the Rev Hezekiah Balch, a pioneering pastor in the mould of   Samuel Doak. Balch, a graduate of Princeton College in New Jersey, arrived in East Tennessee in 1780.

To get lessons up and running, Balch   raised 1,700 dollars and a large number of books during a tour of Philadelphia and New England. The schoolroom adjacent to his home was a basic 32ft by 26 feet two-storey log cabin, with a chimney stack at each end.

Balch died in 1810, to be replaced by the Rev Charles Coffin, and like Tusculum a few miles along in the foothills of the Smokies, the College followed a distinctive ethos until both found it practical to merge.

Today, Tusculum-Greeneville College is a highly reputable American higher education establishment teaching a liberal programme of arts and sciences to students enrolled from a wide area of America.

* Presbyterian churches have been universally called Meeting Houses, whether in the homelands of Scotland and Ulster, or in the new frontier lands of America. From the earliest inception of this creed in the 16th century, Presbyterians did not go to Church, they went to Meeting.

The lay-out and shape of 18th century-early 19th century Presbyterian church buildings in   Pennsylvania, Virginia, North Carolina and Tennessee were remarkably similar to the style of the meeting houses back in Ulster. Even today, the stone-built barn-style meeting houses of Presbyterian congregations at Donegal (Elizabethton, Pennsylvania), Timber Ridge (Lexington, Virginia), Eusebia (Knoxville, Tennessee) and Zion (Maury county, Middle Tennessee) enjoy remarkable parallels with some present church buildings in Northern Ireland.

The raised pulpit with the communion table in front traditionally forms the centrepiece of a Presbyterian church in Scotland, Ireland and the United States.

13

Ulster-born first citizens *of Tennessee*

Thirteen thousand people have registered with the East Tennessee Historical Society in Knoxville as direct descendants of the first families of Tennessee before the state was officially established on June 1, 1796. Among those registered is Texan George Herbert Walker Bush, past President of the United States, whose ancestor William Gault resided in Tennessee in the pre-1796 period.

A large proportion of the first Tennessee families were of Scots-Irish Presbyterian stock, who had either trekked from Pennsylvania down the Great Wagon Road through the Shenandoah Valley of Virginia or moved through the Great Smoky, Blue Ridge and Cumberland Mountains from South Carolina, North Carolina, Georgia and Kentucky.

Hundreds of First Tennesseans have been traced as Ulster-born men and women; thousands more of the early settlers are confirmed either as first, second or third generation Scots-Irish, with parents, grandparents or great grandparents whose birthplace was the north of Ireland; religion Presbyterian; and, who endured the trauma of travelling thousands of miles across the Atlantic in the most horrendous of conditions, in simple wooden ships.

The Scots-Irish diaspora was common currency in the first tentative years of white settlement in Tennessee. The Scots-Irish Presbyterians were the leaders of the white advance into the Tennessee territory when the Holston River and Watauga settlements west of the Allegheny Mountains were forged in the early 1770s, and, over the next two decades, until the state was officially established in 1796, this doggedly determined non-conformist people expanded their remit and influence into every corner of the region.

The Scots-Irish pioneered the first forts and townships in Middle Tennessee, with John Donelson and James Robertson the founders of the city of Nashville (Fort Nashborough) in 1780 after a highly dangerous land and river journey from the Holston River in East Tennessee, and James White, John Adair and George McNutt founders of the city of Knoxville in 1792.

Legendary Tennessee hunter, soldier and politician Davy Crockett belonged to this ethnic group - his family originated in the North Tyrone-East Donegal region of Ulster before emigrating to America. The Crocketts blazed a trail in Tennessee, with Davy, in character, mannerisms and social values, the true persona of the archetypal frontier Scots-Irishman.

Most of the Tennessee counties were first inhabited by the hardy and courageous settler families from the north of Ireland and, tragically, in their bravery and tenacity shown in bitter hostilities with the native American Indian tribes, some paid the supreme sacrifice, while others were left with terrible scars for the rest of their lives.

The distinguished list of known Ulster-born Tennessee first sons and daughters, who opened up this stretch of the American frontier, is a very interesting one, with surnames that can be readily identified with many families who live in Northern Ireland today and who are kinsfolk of those who left for the 'New World' in the 18th century:

- **John Adair** (spouse Eleanor Crawford) - born Co Antrim 1732, settled Knox county 1792.
- **David Adair Sen.** (spouse Mary ("Molly" ——) - born Co Antrim 1730, settled Sullivan county 1787.
- **William Alexander** (spouse Elizabeth King) - born Ireland 1739, settled Greene county 1794.
- **Oliver Alexander** (spouse Margaret Paul) - born Ireland 1732, settled Blount county 1795
- **William Anderson** (spouse Jane Bryan) - born Ireland 1736, settled Sullivan county 1773.
- **Robert Armstrong 11** (spouse Margaret Cunningham) - born Co Antrim 1731, settled Washington county 1783.

- **William Armstrong** 11 (spouse Mary Caldwell) - born Ireland 1712, settled Hawkins county 1780
- **Claudius Bailey** (spouse Margaret Johnston) - born Ireland 1750, settled Greene county 1786.
- **Thomas Bailey** (spouse Elizabeth Weems) - born Londonderry 1760, settled Greene county 1790.
- **Jane Gass Brittain** (spouse James Brittain) - born Ireland 1750, settled Greene county 1794.
- **John Brooks** (spouse Ann Irwin) - born Ireland 1730, settled Knox county 1793.
- **James Brown** (spouse Jane Gillespie) - born Ireland 1738, settled Davidson county 1788.
- **Margaret "Peggy" Fleming Brown** (spouse William Brown) - born Londonderry 1701, settled Davidson county 1793.
- **John Buchanan Sen.** (spouse Jane Trindale) - born Ireland 1704, settled Davidson county 1780.
- **Hugh Cain** - born Ireland 1756, settled Hawkins county 1793.
- **Rachel Calvert** (spouse James Wellington McMahan) - Born Ireland 1755, settled Jefferson county 1790.
- **Robert Campbell** (spouse Leticia Crockett) - born Co Down 1718, settled Hawkins county 1776.
- **Andrew Carithers** (spouse Esther French) - born Ireland 1742, settled Knox county 1795.
- **John Carmichael Sen.** (spouse Susannah McBrayer) - born Ireland 1733, settled Washington county 1784.
- **William Carr** (spouse Martha Harris) - born Ireland 1755, settled Sullivan county 1779.
- **George Cathey** (spouse Ann Price) - born Ireland 1735, settled Sullivan county 1788.
- **Jeremiah Chamberlain** (spouse Margaret Carmichael) - born Ireland 1740, settled Greene county 1790.
- **Ninian Chamberlain** (spouse Janet ——) - born Co Antrim 1719, settled Jefferson county 1795.
- **Higgins Coppinger** (spouse Anna Smith) - born Ireland 1738, settled Sullivan county 1796.
- **John Crockett** (spouse Rebecca Hawkins) - born Ireland 1756, settled Greene county 1776.

- **David Crawford** (spouse Elizabeth Lowrance) - born Londonderry 1755, settled Dyer county 1791.
- **John Crozier** (spouse Hannah Barton) - born Co Fermanagh 1769, settled Knox county 1793.
- **Arabella Goode Cunnynham** (spouse James Cunnyham) - born Ireland 1743, settled Jefferson county 1791.
- **William Henry Cunnyham** (spouse Magdalene Lewis) - born Ireland 1765, settled McMinn county 1796
- **William Dickson** (spouse Eliza Douglas) - born Co Antrim 1775, settled Greene county 1796.
- **Adam Dinsmore** (spouse Elizabeth ———) - born Co Donegal 1760, settled Sullivan county 1778.
- **William Donaldson** (spouse Mary Sweeney) - born Ireland 1738, settled Hawkins county 1790.
- **Hugh Duggan** (spouse Margaret Wilson) - born Ireland 1750, settled Sevier county 1787.
- **Robert Duggan** (spouse Margaret Dunn) - born Ireland 1760, settled Sevier county 1784.
- **Hugh Dunlap** (spouse Susannah Ellis Gilliam) - born Londonderry 1763, settled Knox county 1792.
- **Robert Espy** (spouse Rachel Bell) - born Ireland 1727, settled Davidson county 1790.
- **Nicholas Fain** (spouse Elizabeth Taylor) - born Ireland 1730, settled Washington county 1785.
- **Alexander Ferguson** (spouse Mary Polly McNutt) - born Dunfanaghy, Co Donegal 1768, settled Knox county 1790.
- **Margaret Fleming** (spouse William Brown) - born Ireland 1701, settled Davidson county 1793.
- **Edward Freels** - born Ireland 1752, settled Hawkins county 1787.
- **James Gallaher** (spouse Sarah ———), born Co Donegal 1730, settled Washington county 1783.
- **Josias Gamble** (spouse Ann Ganwell) - born Ireland 1747, settled Blount county 1777.
- **Robert Gamble 11** (spouse Mary McElroy) - born Co Down 1732, settled Knox county 1772.
- **Jacob Gass** (spouse Mary ———) - born Dromore, Co Down 1755, settled Greene county 1783.

- **John Gass** (spouse Margaret ————) - born Co Down 1758, settled Greene county 1783.
- **Samuel Gass** (spouse Rebecca Kerr) - born Co Down 1764, settled Jefferson county 1789.
- **John Gaut Sen.** (spouse Letitia McCall) - born Ireland 1769, settled Jefferson county 1791.
- **Abraham Ghormley** (spouse Elizabeth McAllister) - born Co Tyrone 1758, settled Blount county 1793.
- **Hugh Gilbreath** (spouse Elizabeth Johnston) - born Co Armagh 1742, settled Hawkins county 1793.
- **George Gillespie** (spouse Elizabeth Young) - born Co Antrim 1735, settled Greene county 1794.
- **George Gillespie** (spouse Martha Allen) - born Ireland 1735, settled Washington county 1779.
- **William Glass** (spouse Sarah Pursley) - born Ireland 1725, settled Washington county 1789.
- **Robert Gregg** (spouse Lydia Alice Harrison), - born Ireland 1732, settled Greene county 1794.
- **Adam Guthery** - born Ireland 1750, settled Washington county 1787.
- **James Hamilton Sen** - born Ireland 1720, settled Grainger county 1774.
- **William Hines** (spouse Martha Bright) - born Ireland 1750, settled Knox county 1793.
- **James Houston** (spouse Agnes Wilson) - born Co Antrim 1730, settled Greene county 1783.
- **John Houston** (spouse Sarah Todd) - born Co Antrim 1726, settled Blount county 1795.
- **Samuel Houston** (spouse Elizabeth McCroskey) - born Co Antrim 1725, settled Knox county 1786.
- **David Hughes** (spouse Anna ————) - born Ireland 1757, settled Sullivan county 1777.
- **William Humphrey** (spouse Sarah McClung) - born Co Armagh 1745, settled Blunt county 1787.
- **Henry Johnson** (spouse Rachel Holman) - born Ireland 1783, settled Robertson county 1796.
- **Major John B. Johnston Sen.** (spouse Elizabeth Locke) - born Co Tyrone 1734, settled Davidson county 1790.

- **Alexander Kelly** (spouse Nancy Robinson) - born Co Armagh 1755, settled Knox county 1794.
- **John Kelly** (spouse Margaret McCoy) - born Ireland 1750, settled Greene county 1788.
- **Rev James Kennedy** (spouse Mary Jane Smith) - born Ireland 1768, settled Knox county 1790.
- **Rebeckah Meek Kennedy** (spouse Dr Samuel Kennedy) - born Londonderry 1750, settled Jefferson county 1790.
- **Charles Kilgore** (spouse Winnie Clayton) - born Ireland 1744, settled Greene county 1783.
- **Henry King** (spouse Sarah Shields) - born Ireland 1752, settled Washington county 1783.
- **Robert Kyle** (spouse Leah Brooks) - born Ireland 1740, settled Hawkins county 1788.
- **Andrew Lewis** (spouse Elizabeth Givens) - born Co Donegal 1720.
- **Gilbert Marshall** (spouse Martha Rowan) - born Carnmoney, Co Antrim 1715, settled Davidson county 1786.
- **Nathaniel Maxwell** (spouse Esther Carson) - born Ireland 1741, settled Sullivan county 1789.
- **John McAllister** (spouse Frances Dysart) - born Co Antrim 1737, settled Washington county 1787
- **Solomon McCampbell** (spouse Nancy Berry) - born Ireland 1753, settled Knox county 1790.
- **James McCloud** (spouse Mary Collinsworth) - born Ireland 1765, settled Knox county 1778.
- **Thomas McCrory** (spouse Rachel Shelby Liggett) - born Co Antrim 1766, settled Davidson county 1792.
- **William McGaugh** (spouse Ruth Hill) - born Ireland 1720, settled Davidson county 1780.
- **James McGavock Sen.** (spouse Mary Cloyd) - born Co Antrim 1728, settled Davidson county 1787.
- **David McGill** (spouse Mary Polly McCrary) - born Ireland 1779, settled Roane county 1796.
- **James McMahan** (spouse Rachel Calvert) - born Ireland 1750, settled Sevier county 1796.
- **John McMahon** (spouse Isabelle Barnes) - born Ireland 1728, settled Washington county 1782.

- **Alexander McMillan** (spouse Margaret ————) - born Co Londonderry 1749, settled 1786.
- **John McMillan** (spouse Susannah Beson) - born Ireland 1770, settled Robertson county 1796.
- **George McNutt** (spouses Isabella Callison, Catherine Kain) - born Co Antrim 1751, settled Knox county 1791.
- **William McWhirter** (spouse Elizabeth Ferrier) - born Ireland 1720, settled Davidson county 1787
- **John Minnis** (spouse Nancy Susan McCammon) - born Co Down 1750, settled Blount county 1793.
- **Samuel Patterson** (spouse Martha Ramsey) - born Ireland 1743, settled Davidson county 1794.
- **John Patton** (spouse Mary McKeehan) - born Ireland 1749, settled Carter county 1775.
- **John Peoples** (spouse Hannah ————) - born Ireland 1744, settled Carter county 1796.
- **John Pickens** (spouse Letitia Hannah) - born Belfast 1751, settled Blount County 1796.
- **Thomas Rankin** (spouse Mary Isabel Clendenen) - born Co Londonderry 1724, settled Greene county 1784.
- **Timothy Reagan** (spouse Elizabeth Trigg) - born Ireland 1750, settled Sevier county 1790.
- **James Reynolds** (spouse Mary Bannon) - born Co Louth 1733, settled Hawkins county 1789.
- **Joseph Rhea** (spouse Elizabeth McIlwaine) - born Co Donegal 1715, settled Sullivan county 1775.
- **Matthew Rhea** (spouse Jane Preston) - born Co Donegal 1756, settled Sullivan county 1791.
- **William Rhea** (spouse Elizabeth Breden) - born Co Donegal 1761, settled Sullivan county 1787.
- **William Robinson** (spouse Martha Robertson) - born Ireland 1745, settled Lincoln county 1794.
- **Joseph Rogers** (spouse Mary Amis) - born 1764 Cookstown, Co Tyrone, settled Hawkins county 1782.
- **William Ross** (spouse Jane Allison) - born Ireland 1737, settled Blount county 1790.
- **Bryce Russell** (spouse Jane Thompson) - born Carnmoney, Co Antrim, settled Sullivan county 1794.

- **William Russell** (spouse Sarah Hamilton Henderson) - born Ireland, settled Bounty county 1790.
- **George Rutledge** (spouse Annie Armstrong) - born Co Tyrone 1755, settled Sullivan county 1777.
- **William Rutledge** (spouse Eleanor Caldwell) - born Co Tyrone 1728, settled Sullivan county 1783.
- **Griffith Rutherford** (spouse Mary Elizabeth Graham) - born Ireland 1721, settled Sumner county 1792.
- **Morris Shane** (spouse Pheobe Castleman) - born Ireland 1770, settled Davidson county 1795.
- **John Stirling** (spouse Hannah —————) - born Ireland 1750, settled Knox county 1795.
- **David Stuart** (spouse (Anne Allison) - born Ireland 1765, settled Washington county 1792.
- **Andrew Taylor** (spouse Elizabeth Wilson) - born Co Antrim 1730, settled Carter county 1778.
- **George Tedford** (spouse Jane Hannah) - born Ireland 1753, settled Blount county 1793.
- **James Thompson** (spouse Elizabeth Stum) - born Ireland 1735, settled Davidson county 1780.
- **James Todd** (spouse Sarah Jane Buchanan) - born Ireland 1749, settled Davidson county 1784.
- **John Toole** (spouse Ruth Ann Rankin) - born Belfast 1756, settled Greene county 1788.
- **John Waddell** (spouse Rachel Quee) - born Co Donegal 1736, settled Washington county 1780.
- **John Ward** (spouse Catherine McDaniel) - born Ireland 1741, settled Greene county 1788.
- **Mary Polly Thompson Wear** (spouse Colonel Samuel Wear) - born Co Antrim 1758, settled Sevier county 1796.
- **Robert Wear** (spouse Rebecca Carrell) - born Co Antrim 1715, settled Sevier county 1790.
- **John White** (spouse Ann ———) - born Ireland 1754, settled Washington county 1796.
- **Jason Wilson** (spouse Cynthia Patton) - born Ireland 1749, settled Weakley county 1781.

"How better to honour our forebears than to preserve the record of their pioneering courage."

14

Pioneering Scots-Irish families *of Tennessee*

THE ARMSTRONGS

Co Antrim-born Robert Armstrong 11 and his wife Margaret Cunningham were first citizens of Knox county in Tennessee. At the age of four in 1735, Robert came to America with his parents Robert and Alice Calhoun Armstrong and after living for a short time in Pennsylvania the family moved to Abbeville in South Carolina via the Shenandoah Valley of Virginia.

Robert 11 became a Revolutionary War lieutenant in the First South Carolina Regiment and by 1784 he was living at Washington county, North Carolina (now in East Tennessee). Margaret Cunningham was born in the Shenandoah Valley, of a Scots-Irish family, and they had seven children.

A nephew Robert Houston was the first sheriff of Knox county and later was a Tennessee secretary of state.

THE CAMPBELLS

This Co Down family - five brothers (Archibald, Alexander, William, Colin and Robert) and a sister (Catherine) - emigrated to Philadelphia in 1725 and over a period of 50 years they moved to Virginia and Tennessee.

Robert Campbell married Leticia Crockett, who is believed to have travelled from Belfast with her family on the same ship as the

Campbells. The couple lived in Prince Edward county and Rockbridge county, Virginia and at Carter's Valley near Rogersville at Hawkins county in East Tennessee from 1776. They had 11 children and one of the sons Andrew was killed by Indians in 1785. A son-in-law Joseph Long, who married Elizabeth Campbell, died at the Battle of Kings Mountain 1780.

THE CUNNYNGHAMS

James and Arabella (Good) Cunnyngham emigrated from Ulster in 1769 and moved to the Shenandoah Valley of Virginia from Pennsylvania. James remained a strong Episcopalian until his death in 1786, but after his widow and their six children moved to East Tennessee (in the region of the French Broad River), the family turned to the Methodist faith and helped establish the Pine Wesleyan Chapel near Dandridge in Jefferson county.

George Cunnyngham, a son, was murdered in 1792 by Cherokee Indians in an ambush typical of the period and several other members of the Pine Chapel congregation died or were seriously injured in atrocities. The 21-year-old daughter and eight-year-old son of congregational leader Amos Lewis and his wife Mary were captured, scalped and killed.

Arabella Cunnyngham and her two daughters Arabella and Charlotte devoted much of their time to establishing the Pine Chapel. Arabella was married to George Turnley, a revolutionary soldier and noted Indian fighter from a Scots-Irish family who had lived in Virginia

The Rev W. G. E. Cunnyngham, a great grandson of James and Arabella Cunnyngham, was a missionary to China and the Sunday school secretary of the Methodist Episcopal Church of the South. His father Jesse was one of four commissioners who laid out Monroe county, Tennessee into districts.

The Cunnynghams (Conynghams-Cunninghams) are a distinguished Ulster-Scots family and Conyngham's Regiment served with King William 111 at the Battle of the Boyne in 1690. The Regiment became the 6th Inniskilling Dragoons in 1751.

Methodism on the American frontier, as practised at Pine Chapel, had distinctive symbols with its camp meetings and circuit rider in the mould of English founder John Wesley. The circuit rider was the ministry of a preacher, his horse, sandbags and Bible, which, very often, the evangelist could not read, but knew from memory. The circuit rider was the preacher of the long and lonely road extending hundreds of miles over mountains and through valleys. Some circuit riders had very little academic background, yet through experience of the ways of the frontier settlers and a finely honed sense of oratorical preaching style, they conveyed a gospel message to the settler families which was simple but effective.

While Presbyterianism was the dominant Protestant denomination in the 18th Appalachian territories, Methodism made significant inroads in Tennessee, Virginia and Kentucky, under the crusading leadership of Bishop Francis Ashbury, an English-born cleric influenced by the Calvinist teachings of John and Charles Wesley.

In 1780, at the height of the Revolutionary War, Francis Ashbury rode down the Great Wagon Road to preach to Methodists in Virginia, the Carolinas and Tennessee. After preaching at Haw, North Carolina, he wrote: "I dwell as among briers, thorns and scorpions." It was a route he and other Methodist circuit rider preachers was to take many times in the several decades that were to follow.

In 1796 church reports indicated 725 Methodists belonging to two circuits in Tennessee and South West Virginia: Holston and New River. By 1802, there were 3,000 Methodists operating in five circuits in the region: two in South West Virginia (New River and Clinch) and three in East Tennessee (Holston, Nolichucky and French Broad. The dramatic increase was clearly attributable to the great camp meeting revivals of 1800.

Methodism demonstrated an ability to stick with the task of evangelising a people eager to hear the word of God; to adapt in the difficult surroundings of the frontier and to meet human needs. The Church, proclaiming John Wesley's watchword "friends of all, enemies of none", even succeeded eventually in building bridges through Christian love with the Cherokee tribes who had long been their enemies.

THE DINSMORES

Adam and Elizabeth Dinsmore left Templemore parish in Co Donegal about 1775 and in 1784 the couple received 380 acres of land at Sullivan county in North Carolina in what was to become East Tennessee. The 1790 census showed some of the Dinsmore family at Montgomery county in North Carolina. Adam died in Alabama after moving there with son David and his family.

THE DUGGANS

Revolutionary Army sergeant Robert Duggan was one of the first settlers of Sevier county in Tennessee after the land had been opened up through the treaty of Dumplin with the Cherokees. Robert's father Hugh was born in the north of Ireland and he lived in Virginia for a long period before the move to Tennessee.

THE DUNLAPS

Hugh Dunlap, born in Londonderry in 1769, established the second store in Knoxville, having arrived with goods from Philadelphia in 1792. He married Susannah Gilliam, daughter of a French Huguenot who had settled in Knox county.

The couple's eldest son Richard Gilliam Dunlap served as an escort to Andrew Jackson during the Seminole Indian War in Florida in 1817-18. He was a general in the Tennessee militia and, after the Cherokee Removal Treaty had been officially declared by President Andrew Jackson, Dunlap and his troops policed the Cherokee people in Tennessee, North Carolina and Georgia in case of an uprising. None happened, the militia company was disbanded in 1836 and Dunlap was given to the view that the Cherokees tribes were in more need of protection than the white population.

Disenchanted by Jackson's Indian removal policies, Richard Dunlap said: "I will never aid at the point of a bayonet a treaty made against the will and authority of the Cherokee people."

As a politician, Dunlap was a Knox county representative to the Tennessee legislature and and he was the author of a statute under which a system of public schools was first established in the state.

In 1837, Dunlap moved to Texas, then an independent republic, and he was appointed treasurer of the republic and minister to the United States. A brother James T. was comptroller of the treasury of

Tennessee and two other brothers, Hugh White and William C, were judges in West Tennessee.

The headstone on the graves of Hugh and Susannah Gilliam Dunlap says: "They assisted in the laying of the foundation of civilisation in Tennessee from the eastern to the western border and were the parents of sons distinguished in their native state and in Louisiana, Mississippi and Texas."

THE FAINS

Nicholas Fain, born in Ireland in 1730 of a French Huguenot family, emigrated with his English-born wife Elizabeth Taylor and after living for a few years at Chester county, Pennsylvania moved to Wolf Creek on the south fork of the Holston River in south west Virginia. He finally settled at Knob Creek, Washington county, Tennessee close to the first frontier town of Jonesboro.

In the Revolutionary War, Nicholas was a leading patriot and he received commendation for special services. Five of his sons - Samuel, John (a captain), William, Thomas and Ebenezer - fought at the Battle of Kings Mountain in October, 1780. Another son David was killed by Indians.

In Ireland, Nicholas Fain was an Anglican, but when he reached Tennessee he was a Baptist. Tradition says he was noted for his religious zeal, being converted by the St John's gospel chapter 5 verse 40 - "Ye will not come to Me, that ye might have life". Most of the descendants were either Methodist or Presbyterian.

THE GAMBLES

Robert Gamble, born in Co Down in 1732, was an Indian fighter and Revolutionary War soldier in south western Virginia and had distinguished service under Colonel William Christian in the Cherokee expedition of 1776. Robert married Mary McElroy, also of Co Down stock, in Augusta county, Virginia in 1764 and the family moved to East Tennessee in the 1780s.

John Gamble, a Scots-Irish kinsman who lived in Augusta county, was also a revolutionary soldier, with the 13th Virginia regiment.

Robert and John Gamble may also have been kin to North Carolina soldier Martin Gambill, as the spelling of surnames at the time very often deviated.

Gambill, a first lieutenant in the Continental Army, was wounded at the Battle of Kings Mountain in October, 1780 and after the war he was elected to the North Carolina legislature.

THE GHORMLEYS

Co Tyrone Presbyterian couple Hugh and Catherine Covington Ghormley came to America in May, 1759 with their five-month-old son Abraham and they settled in Cumberland county, Pennsylvania. Abraham, the eldest of a family of 10, was given a classical education and acquired a lot of property in Pennsylvania. He served as a ranger in the Revolutionary War and when he married Scottish lass Elizabeth McAlister in 1788, they moved to Tennessee and raised 10 children.

The Ghormleys developed friendly relationships with the Cherokee Indians in North Carolina and Tennessee with millwright Hugh Ghormley, son of Abraham, grounding meal from corn for the tribes. Hugh's four sons Samuel, Joseph Jasper, Michael and Jesse are believed to have been the first white children born in Cherokee county, North Carolina, then the capital of the Cherokee nation.

Michael Ghormley became highly proficient in the Cherokee language and he learned from the tribes their thrifty way of living and their secrets of nature. But despite the friendly attitude that developed, the Cherokees continually refused to sell the Ghormleys any land in Cherokee county upon which to establish a homestead and after eight years they returned to the established white settlements at Maryville in Blount county.

THE GILBREATHS (GALBRAITHS)

Hugh Gilbreath, a native of Co Armagh, emigrated to America after running away from home when only 14. He landed in Pennsylvania and married Elizabeth Johnston, who was also born in Ireland, and they moved on to East Tennessee where they acquired 400 acres on the Holston River at Hawkins county in 1793.

A few years later the family was resident in the neighbouring Blount county. Hugh's son, John Fisher Gilbreath was a Methodist minister, said to be "mighty in prayer", and he was one of the founders of the Hiwasse College at Monroe county, Tennessee. Interestingly, John Fisher's name on his gravestone is spelt Galbraith. Later, family members served as Confederates in the American Civil War.

THE GILLESPIES

This Co Antrim family is traced to George and Elizabeth Gillespie who emigrated from Ulster to America in 1740. Colonel George Gillespie, a grandson, married Ann Neilson, a member of a Scots-Irish family from Warm Springs, North Carolina, and he owned a 1,000-acre plantation on the Tennessee River known as "Euchee Old Fields."

Colonel Gillespie, a militia leader, was very active in the public affairs of East Tennessee and he served as justice of the peace and sheriff of Washington county. A son Robert Neilson Gillespie was a noted businessman and doctor in Rhea county, while another son Robert was president of the Tennessee Academy.

Another Gillespie (Gillespy) family - James and Jennet and their three sons and a   daughter - also emigrated from Ulster to Pennsylvania in 1740, settling Augusta county in the Shenandoah Valley of Virginia. James helped found the Tinkling Springs Presbyterian Church in 1741 and with his three sons John, James and William fought in the French-Indian war. The sons were also revolutionary war soldiers.

Later, tragedy was to hit the family at their family fort in Blount county, East Tennessee. James Gillespy, son of John, was massacred in an Indian attack in October, 1788 and some members of the family were taken captive. Five years later, James Gillespy Jun. and one of his sons were massacred in another attack on the fort. Another son was captured by the tribesmen, but released a month later on the ransom payment of a quantity of leather and a horse.

These Gillespys were prominent people in Blunt county, with James, son of James Jun. , a local magistrate, Presbyterian elder and member of the Tennessee legislature. His son Dr James Houston Gillespy was an eminent physician of the day and owner of 10,000 acres of mountain and forest land in East Tennessee. He was a leading Confederate in the region during the American Civil War.

THE GLASSES

Donegal man William Glass sailed the oceans of the world for 20 years before he finally decided in 1759 to put down his roots in America. Glass, born at Dunkaneilley about 1724, went to sea as a 16-year-old after a quarrel with his brother Matthew over the right to inherit the family homestead and family records confirm he reached India and South Africa on his travels.

William Glass had a brief stay in Pennsylvania and during his settlement in Orange county, Virginia he married Sarah Purselly, who was also of a Scots-Irish family. In the revolutionary war, Glass fought at the battle of Brandywine in 1777 and, after a period out of service, he enlisted again as a resident of Washington county in East Tennessee in the Watauga militia of General Isaac Shelby.

At the battle of Kings Mountain in 1780 he was injured by a musket shot over the right eye. He returned to farming and is reputed to have planted the first apple orchard in Washington county. He and his wife Sarah had 13 children.

THE HOUSTONS

James Houston, a kinsman of Governor Sam Houston, was a citizen of Tennessee from about 1773, having moved first from Augusta county in the Shenandoah Valley, and then from Roanoke in south western Virginia. This second generation Co Antrim Presbyterian married and his wife Agnes Wilson settled in Greene county, then part of North Carolina, and James played a leading role in the establishment of the government of the new state of Franklin, which only lasted four years. Governor John Sevier appointed him state sheriff and he also served as major of the Franklin militia.

Houston acquired 640 acres on the south side of the Nolichucky River that became known as Houston's Valley, and there he built a large two-storey log home, and a small log church, which was to become the Pine Springs Missionary Baptist Church.

The Rev Samuel Houston, another Shenandoah Valley kinsman of Governor Sam and son of John and Sarah Todd Houston, was an early Presbyterian pastor in East Tennessee, ministering for six years from 1783 to Providence congregation in Washington county. He graduated from Liberty Hall College in Lexington, but the start of his church ministry was postponed while he soldiered in the Revolutionary War.

Houston was one of the ministers who set up the presbytery of Abingdon and he returned to Virginia to serve several churches and establish a classical school. He became a trustee of Liberty Hall-Washington College. Margaret Houston, a sister, became the Rev Samuel Doak's second wife on the death of her husband Alexander McEwen. Doak, whose first wife Esther died after 30-odd years marriage, was a ministerial colleague of the Rev Samuel Houston in East Tennessee.

THE KELLYS

Alexander Kelly was born in Co Armagh about 1750 and was brought to America by his parents in his infancy. Alexander, as a young man living at Greenbriar in Virginia, joined the 9th Virginia Regiment on July 9, 1776 and served through the Revolutionary War.

When he moved to the Tennessee country, Alexander served as a lieutenant colonel in the Knox county militia and emerged prominent in business and political life in the Knoxville area. His considerable business interests are confirmed by the fact that in 1792 the Knox county court ordered roads to be laid from Knoxville to his mill at Nine Mile Creek.

Alexander Kelly was appointed in 1794 as a delegate to the Tennessee territorial legislature and when the state was set up in 1796 he was returned as a senator from Blount county. Kelly was one of the first to enter land on the Tennessee River in Marion county - in 1824. His holding extended to almost 3,000 acres at Sequatchie Valley, but soon after moving to the region he was drowned in the Sequatchie River.

John Kelly, Alexander's eldest son, married Nancy Mayo, a North Carolina family of Scots-Irish descent, and with their two young children they dangerously moved down the Tennessee River in a flat boat to the mouth of Battle Creek while the Indians were still in control of that region.

In 1826, John Kelly was granted a charter by the Tennessee state to build a turnpike road to Ross's Landing (Chattanooga) and he constructed the first bridge across the Sequatchie River. He was also the first to advocate the building of a road around the base of Look-Out Mountain, following the route of the N.C.&St.L. Railroad, and he and his son-in-law Ignatius Hall had a government contract to remove obstructions from the Tennessee River.

Politically, John Kelly was a Whig and he was a member of the Tennessee Constitutional Convention of 1834, serving as circuit court judge. He belonged to Cumberland Presbyterian Church and he and his wife, a Methodist, had 13 children.

THE KENNEDYS

The Rev James Kennedy came to America with his mother Rebeckah Meak Kennedy after his father Samuel, a military medical officer, died in Ireland in 1788. Their home, a log cabin on the site of a creek bank orchard, was close to White's fort in an area that was to emerge as Knoxville.

About 1790, the Rev Kennedy settled on the north side of the French Broad River. He was educated for the ministry in Edinburgh and was a Presbyterian in the Seceder tradition.

THE KERRS

David Kerr was a revolutionary soldier in the 10th Regiment of the Continental Line, 2nd Virginia Brigade and after the war he bought an extensive tract of land on the Nolichucky River, then Dumplin Creek, Greene county in Franklin state (now East Tennessee).

Kerr's daughter Rebecca married Samuel Gass, who had emigrated from Co Down in 1785 and Gass purchased 100 acres for 200 pounds at Dumplin Creek from his father-in-law. Both the Kerr and Gass homesteads were under constant attack from marauding Chereokee tribes and families in the region were forced to seek refuge in Henry

The Upper Octorara Presbyterian Session House in Eastern Pennsylvania, erected about 1748 by a congregation of Scots-Irish settlers who founded the church in 1720.

The third church at Upper Octorara in Eastern Pennsylvania, erected 1821. The first church was built of logs in the early 1720s and, when it was burned down, it was replaced by a stone building, probably about 1748.

Union Academy in Knox County, East Tennessee - "The Log College".

The first Maryville College at Blount County, East Tennessee, founded by Scots-Irish frontier cleric the Rev. Isaac Anderson.

The Rev. Samuel Doak, son of a Co. Antrim-born couple, and the Martin Academy he founded in East Tennessee in 1783. The Academy was later known as Washington College.

Frontier settlers gather for a religious camp meeting which were popular in Tennessee and Kentucky in the late 18th - early 19th centuries.

Worshippers at prayer during an American frontier camp meeting.

Portrait of Davy Crockett made in 1831.

President Andrew Jackson, the son of a Co. Antrim-born couple. He served two terms in the White House.

A Frontiersman at peace with the world.
(Picture: H. David Wright, Nashville)

James Robertson and his Scots-Irish compatriots from the Watauga region of East Tennessee cross the frozen Cumberland River on their perilous journey to Fort Nashborough (Nashville) in the winter of 1779-80. (Picture H. David Wright, Nashville)

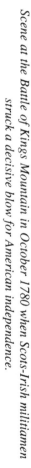

Scene at the Battle of Kings Mountain in October 1780 when Scots-Irish militiamen struck a decisive blow for American independence.

The scene at Ninety-Six on South Carolina soil in May, 1781, when the Scots-Irish were heavily involved in another crucial Revolutionary War battle.

President Ulysses S. Grant, commander of the Union Army during the American Civil War. Grant's mother, Hannah Simpson was descended from the Simpson family of Dergenagh near Dungannon in Co. Tyrone.

President Chester Alan Arthur, whose grandfather and father,
Baptist pastor William Arthur, emigrated from Dreen near
Cullybackey, Co. Antrim in 1801.

The Museum of Appalachia at Norris, East Tennessee contains a collection of more than 30 authentic log cabin buildings, including a gristmill, a school, a church, barns, smokehouse and cabins - all dating from the late 18th century to the early 1900s.

*Gray's printing shop at Strabane, Co. Tyrone, where John Dunlap, the
printer of the American Declaration of Independence in 1776, learned his
trade before he emigrated to America in 1741. James Wilson, grandfather
of President Woodrow Wilson, also worked at Gray's printing shop.
He emigrated from Co. Tyrone in 1807.
(Picture: The National Trust, Northern Ireland)*

*President Benjamin Harrison, whose two great grandfathers,
James Irwin and William McDowell, were Ulstermen.*

Station, a small fort used for common defence. These families belonged to the pioneering Hopewell Presbyterian Church.

THE McMAHONS (McMAHANS)

John McMahon, born in the north of Ireland in 1728, is credited with being the owner of the first house in Tennessee with a stone chimney and a shingle roof, built in 1774. The house on several hundred acres of land in Washington county, then part of North Carolina, was totally isolated in a region where the dangers to the white settlers from hostile Cherokee Indian tribes were all too apparent.

When it was erected there was no other house (and only one cabin) west of it to the Mississippi River, except the military building at Chickasaw Bluffs near Memphis, a distance of about 500 miles. The cabin, belonging to a John Clark, was on the Nolichucky River, west of where the town of Jonesboro in East Tennessee now stands.

Several McMahon families were living in south west Virginia from the early-1770s and when John and Isabella McMahon and their family reached the Watauga Valley most of the land had been taken up and they were forced to settle on the most westerly frontier perimeter, beyond the gap of Sycamore Shoals, in the area of present-day Johnson City.

John McMahon's nearest neighbour was Joseph Young, who resided five miles east of Jonesboro, and on at least two occasions during Indian troubles members of the McMahon family had to flee back to the relative safety of Abingdon in Virginia.

Rosannah McMahon, John's daughter, married Samuel Fain, son of Irish-born Nicholas Fain, who had settled on the forks of the Holston River in Washington county. Militiaman Samuel fought in the Revolutionary War battles of Kings Mountain and Mount Pleasant and with the McMahons helped fend off numerous Indian attacks.

The McMahons belonged to First Jonesboro Presbyterian Church and when John died, his son John moved to Kentucky. The McMahon family homestead was acquired by David Deaderick, a pioneer merchant of Jonesboro.

James McMahan (McMahon), another emigrant from Ulster, settled with his wife Rachel Calvert and family in Sevier county, East

Tennessee, and in 1796 James was awarded the first 25 acres for the township known as "The Forks of the Little Pigeon", which today is Pigeon Forge, home of American country singer Dolly Parton.

James was a close associate of Colonel John Sevier, in turn governor of the lost state of Franklin and Tennessee and a United States Congressman from North Carolina. The McMahans reared 13 children on their vast expanse of farmland in the foothills of the Great Smoky Mountains.

Today, a McMahan Indian Mound is sited on the Forks of the River Pathway at Sevierville, dedicated to the memory of the Mississippian and Overhill Cherokee tribes who roamed the region from 200 A.D. to the late 1770s when white families like the McMahans, Fains, Duggans, Alexanders and Wears arrived to stake land claims.

The Treaty of Dumplin Creek of June 10, 1785, conducted between the white settler leaders led by John Sevier, David Kennedy and Ebenezer Alexander and the Cherokee Indians led by "king" Ancoo of Chota, authorised that all of Jefferson, Hamblen, Sevier, Knox and Blount counties, in what was to become 11 years later part of the new state of Tennessee, be opened up to settler homesteads.

The Treaty outlined that "liberal compensation" be made to the Cherokees for the land that had been ceded and granted by them to the white people on the south side of the Holston and French Broad Rivers to the region of the Tennessee River.

Initial difficulties arose with the North Carolina legislature ignoring the Treaty provisions and the Indians also repudiating some of the terms. But within three years more than 1,000 families, most of them of Scots-Irish origin, had moved in and established homesteads on these historic Indian lands.

It was very dangerous territory for the white settlers and, as a means of protection and communal vantage point, they established fort stations or blockhouses. The McGaughey, McTeer, McCroskey, Hunter and Houston forts on the trail between Sevierville and Knoxville acted as safety havens for the various families.

Historian David Ramsey wrote of the period: "Boys became men, women turned soldiers, assisting in the defense of the family and home. Vigilance and heroism, fearlessness and energy, characterised the entire population. Could a diagram be drawn, accurately designating every spot signalized by an Indian massacre, surprise of depredation, or courageous attack, defense, pursuit or victory by the whites; or fort, or battlefield, or personal encounter, the whole of that section of country could be studded by delineations of such incidents. Nearly every spring, ford, path, farm. trail or house, in its first settlement, was once the scene of danger, exposure, attack, exploit, achievement or death."

Many of the Indian tribes displaced in the Tennessee land treaties eventually moved west to new territories, but some maintained settlements in the Great Smoky Mountains, where today their descendants live in the township of Cherokee, which straddles the borders of North Carolina and Tennessee.

THE MARSHALLS

Gilbert Marshall from Carnmoney, Co Antrim and his wife Martha Rowan emigrated to Pennsylvania in 1750 and, after spending three years in Lancaster county, they moved into the Shenandoah Valley of Virginia to settle on 250 acres of land at Back Creek in Albermarle county. On this homestead ten Marshall children were born.

Marshall and his grown sons enlisted in the Virginia militia at the outbreak of war in 1776 and in 1781 he was given a land grant of 400 acres in lieu of revolutionary service at Lincoln county, Virginia, which today is now part of Kentucky. He and the family finally settled in Middle Tennessee in 1789, on land at White's Creek near Nashville.

THE MINNISES

Few 18th century Ulster emigrants to America returned to their homeland, so arduous was the sea trip back across the Atlantic and so marked was the difference in life styles between the New World and the old country. Co Down man John Minnis made the journey back after spending a decade and more in America in the years before and during the Revolutionary War. His mission in Ireland - to find a wife.

John, the son of Samuel and Mary (Bittles) Minnis, joined the militia shortly after his arrival in Philadelphia and he served as a sergeant in the 13th and 2nd Pennsylvania regiments, fighting at the battles of Brandywine, Trenton and Princeton. After the war, John Minnis returned to Ireland and there he married Nancy Susan McCammon, of Co Tyrone, in 1787.

The couple headed to America with Nancy's three brothers John, Samuel and Thomas McCammon and they settled on 600 acres in Blount County, Tennessee.

John and Nancy had eight children, six sons and two daughters, the most notable of whom were Thomas, a soldier in the New Orleans war and a judge in Tennessee and Missouri, and William, a Presbyterian minister.

The Rev William Minnis was acknowledged as a distinguished scholar, a bold fearless preacher and a pastor with energy of character and an ardent thirst for education. The Minnis family were of the Seceder or Covenanter Presbyterian tradition and William, a graduate of Maryville College, ministered for 37 years at Westminster Presbyterian Church near Dandridge and in neighbouring congregations in East Tennessee.

John B. Minnis, William's son, was a distinguished Union Army soldier in the Civil War, operating as inspector of Tennessee troops on the staff of Andrew Johnson, then state military governor. After the War, John B. served in the Tennessee state legislature as representative for Jefferson county.

THE PATTERSONS

Samuel Patterson who emigrated to America as a 16-year-old with his family was an early settler in Tennessee, after living in Lancaster county, Pennsylvania and Mecklenburg county, North Carolina. Samuel was a signer of the Mecklenburg Declaration of 1775, which was the forerunner of the Declaration of Independence, and after service in the Revolutionary War he set his sights on land in Middle Tennessee.

By the turn of the century, the Pattersons had acquired several thousand acres in Davidson, Sumner, Wilson and Bedford counties, with Samuel in full control of affairs until his death in 1815.

A son, Captain Andrew Patterson, served with Andrew Jackson at the Battle of New Orleans in 1815.

THE PICKENS

John Pickens was born in Belfast in 1751 and he met his wife Letitia Hannah in the south west region of Virginia near the Tennessee border. They married about 1783 and later moved on to several hundred acres of land on the Middle Fort of the Holston River in East Tennessee.

Pickens was an extensive farmer and animal stockman and his land ownership extended to Blount county in the Great Smoky Mountain region. Both he and his wife are buried in the Eusebia Presbyterian Church cemetery near Maryville.

THE RANKINS

This family from the Londonderry-Donegal area was amongst the hundreds of Ulster immigrants who settled in the New England colonies and Pennsylvania from 1718 to 1720. Brothers James, Hugh and Adam Rankin, whose Scottish-born grandfather Alexander and father William defended Londonderry in the 1688-89 Siege, were in Chester county, Pennsylvania in 1720 and, after moving down the Shenandoah Valley, family members turned up in Tennessee and Kentucky.

The Rev Adam Rankin, a grandson of Adam, went along the Wilderness Road into Kentucky in 1784 and established a Presbyterian church where the city of Lexington now stands.

Another Rankin cleric, the Rev John, was one of a number of pastors who led the Great Revival in Kentucky-Tennessee at the turn of the 18th-19th centuries and he was the pastor of the Presbyterian church at Ripley, Ohio for 44 years.

He was a great grandson of Donegal-born John Rankin, who with his wife Jane McIlwee and children moved out to Pennsylvania in 1727.

Members of the family settled in Augusta county, Virginia and later in Green County, Tennessee. Seven grandsons of John Rankin fought alongside General George Washington in the Revolutionary War; four great grandsons were with General Andrew Jackson at the Battle of New Orleans and later generations fought in the Civil War. Rankin family members were also involved in the Hopewell Presbyterian Church at Dandridge in East Tennessee.

In the United States census of 1790, 75 Rankin families were listed, all believed to have an Ulster-Scots link. Thirty-seven lived in Pennsylvania, nine in North Carolina, eight in Maine, seven in Maryland, six in South Carolina, four in New York, two in New Hampshire and two in Vermont.

* Alexander Rankin, who was at the Siege of Londonderry with his son William, was a signator to the petition of "thanks to Almighty God, and to William, Prince of Orange, for his timely assistance in raising the Siege in the city in August, 1689."

THE REYNOLDS

James and Mary Bannon Reynolds lived in the Creggan parish that straddled counties Armagh, Monaghan and Louth before they emigrated to America about 1780. All seven of their children were born in Ireland and the family settled in Hawkins and Knox counties in Tennessee after passing through Pennsylvania. They belonged to Washington Pike Presbyterian Church in Knox county.

THE RUSSELLS

Bryce Russell and his sister Isabelle Helene from Carnmoney, Co Antrim were among the first Scots-Irish settlers in the Shenandoah Valley, with Bryce pioneering the Tennessee country from 1773. Isabelle Helene married Co Antrim-born the Rev John Craig in Pennsylvania in 1744 and they moved to the Shenandoah when Craig was appointed minister of Tinkling Springs Presbyterian Church in Augusta county.

On moving to the Holston River area, Bryce and son Bryce Jun. signed the Watauga petition to the state of North Carolina for the founding of Franklin county which aborted after a few years to become Sullivan county, Tennessee.

The Russell fort house came under regular attack by Indians and, in one incident when Bryce was away from home, sons George and Hugh were killed and his wife Jane was scalped and left for dead. She survived, but her twin daughters Rachel and Isabella were captured along with a black slave and taken to the Canadian border.

There, with the help of another captive Frenchman Raif Naylor, the two girls escaped and returned home after two years. Raif and Isabella were married and had a family, but family records confirm that one evening Raif stepped outside the house to smoke. He disappeared and was never seen again.

THE RUTLEDGES

This distinguished Ulster family can be traced back to George and Nelly Gamble Rutledge from Co Tyrone whose five children William, Thomas, John, Jane and Catherine emigrated to America in 1763.

The Rutledge brothers and sisters and their families settled at Augusta county in the Shenandoah Valley of Virginia and they were a prominent family in the Tinkling Springs Presbyterian Church before they moved on to North Carolina and East Tennessee in 1777.

William Rutledge had married Eleanor Caldwell, from Co Cavan, before they left Ireland and their son George (born in Co Tyrone in 1755) was a militia officer in the Revolutionary War, earning particular recognition for his service at the Battle of Kings Mountain.

George Rutledge became brigadier general and state militia commander when John Sevier was appointed the first Tennessee governor in 1796 and he represented Sullivan county in the Tennessee legislature. His wife Annie Armstrong belonged to a Co Fermanagh family who had also moved to the Shenandoah Valley. A Tennessee county is named in George Rutledge's memory.

A distant kinsman of the George Rutledge family from Co Tyrone was Edward Rutledge, who helped draft the Declaration of Independence in 1776 and was a militia officer during the Revolutionary War. Edward, a Charleston lawyer, was governor of South Carolina from 1798 to 1800.

His bother John, also a lawyer in Charleston, served for two years as the first governor of South Carolina and he was chief justice of the state's supreme court. In 1795, President George Washington nominated him for chief justice of the US Supreme Court, but the Senate refused to confirm the appointment because of Rutledge's opposition to Jay's Treaty, which, going against Washington's advice, advocated closer links in the role of land and sea forces of both the American Administration and Britain.

THE STERRETTS (STIRRATTS)

This Ulster Presbyterian family which can be traced back to Benjamin Sterrett came to America in 1730, settling at Lancaster county, Pennsylvania. Benjamin has three sons Cairns, John and James and a daughter Mary and their families spread to South Carolina, North Carolina and Tennessee.

A grandson of the original immigrant, Benjamin Sterritt (Sterrett), is recorded as one of the heroes at the Battle of Kings Mountain in October, 1780.

THE STEWARTS

During the latter part of the 18th century it was against the law for white settlers to settle on Indian land and Irish-born William Stewart fell foul of the authorities when he did this in Tennessee. United States regular soldiers came and burned William's log cabin and destroyed his crops at Looney's Creek, Marian county close to Chatanooga and, after much haggling, he was forced to move to lands in the neighbouring Bledsoe county, and then to Blount county.

William and Elizabeth Stewart had eight children and the family trek to Tennessee over a period of five years was via Baltimore in Maryland to Abingdon in South Western Virginia. A son John fought in the War of 1812.

THE THOMPSONS

Captain James Thompson was an early Tennessee pioneer of second generation Ulster stock who lived on the headwaters of Richland Creek, a few miles south of Nashville. He had previously lived in Mecklenburg County, North Carolina and on the Watauga settlement in East Tennessee and commanded a militia company at the Battle of Island Flats during the first skirmish of the Revolutionary War west of the Allegeny Mountains.

Thompson, married to Elizabeth Stump, came to East Tennessee in 1780 with his kinsmen Absolom, Charles, Robert, Andrew and Thomas Thompson and they all signed the Cumberland Compact which confirmed local autonomy in the region. He acquired 640 acres a few miles south of Nashville (then Fort Nashborough) and on this land Thompson built a chinked and daubed log cabin surrounded with a yard fence, which became known as Thompson's Station.

Tragically, the Thompson family suffered grievously at the hands of hostile Creek Indians, with James and Elizabeth, two sons Robert and John and invalid daughter Elizabeth dying in attacks. On June 2, 1791, the Indians attacked Thompson's Station and killed John while he was working on the cornfield near the fort.

Then on February 25, 1792, about 30 Creek Indians arrived at the station and murdered four of the family: John and Elizabeth, son Robert and daughter Elizabeth, who was found down the trail from the fort, scalped and left for dead in the snow. She died within a few hours.

The Indians took as prisoners another daughter Alice and a neighbour Mrs Peter Caffrey and her two-year-old son and held them at a Creek settlement on the Tallapoosa River. John Riley, an Irish-born trader, offered to ransom the two women, but it took two years of hard bargaining with the Indians before their releases were granted.

Alice Thompson's freedom was gained by a barter of eight hundred weight of dressed deer skins and it was said that she was treated well by her captors. A similar deal had to be offered to the tribes for Mrs Caffrey's release and, three years on, the Caffrey boy was returned to his mother, a child grown in Indian customs.

Alice Thompson married Edmund Collinsworth in Davidson county, Tennessee in 1795 and a son James was an attorney, who was one of the commissioners at Washington DC when the United States was urging Mexico to recognise independence for Texas in the 1830s. He was distinguished at the bar in both Texas and Tennessee. Two other brothers John and George were educated at West Point and moved to Texas as soldiers and surveyors.

THE WEARS (WEIRS)

This family belonged to the group of Bann Valley (East Londonderry-North Antrim) Presbyterians who moved to New

England in the summer of 1718, settling at Nutfield in New Hampshire, a township later to be known as Londonderry. Robert Weir was a first Nutfield settler and his son Robert a generation later established the family tree at Augusta county in Virginia.

Colonel Samuel Wear, who built the first home at Pigeon Forge in East Tennessee in 1790, is believed to be directly descended from the Weirs of New Hampshire and Augusta county, with some genealogical papers claiming he was the son of Robert Weir Jun.

The Wear (Weir-Weer-Ware) family name has been subjected to various spellings, as was common on the American frontier in the 18th century, and obviously the connections of Colonel Samuel Wear and his brother John were quite happy with their version.

Samuel Wear began his military life in 1777 when appointed ensign in the Augusta county, Virginia militia, serving alongside John Sevier, the first governor of Tennessee. Wear fought throughout the Revolutionary War - at Yorktown, Kings Mountain and New Orleans - and when hostilities ceased he actively participated in the early life of Tennessee. He was also clerk of the state of Franklin, which aborted after a few years, and a colonel in the state militia.

When Samuel Wear moved to what is now Sevier county, Tennessee, very few white settlers lived in the region south of the French Broad River and, with the help of his black slave Frank, he staked out a fertile homestead on land granted to him for service in the Revolutionary War.

His log blockhouse in the foothills of the Great Smoky Mountains became Wear's Fort, a focal point and refuge for the Wear family and their neighbours from the raids of the Cherokee Indians who had still not relinquished title to this section of the American frontier.

Thirty miles to the south west of Wear's Fort on the Little Tennessee River were the tribal camps of the Overhill Cherokees, and the fort lay directly in the way of the Great Indian War Path from Virginia, which led from the French Broad River through Pigeon Forge.

On June 19, 1793 Wear's Fort was attacked by a large Cherokee force and a report in the Knoxville Gazette, Tennessee's first newspaper, confirmed the destruction of "growing corn, the theft and killing of horses, cattle and hogs, as well as the partial destruction of Wear's Mill, and the theft of meal from the mill."

"Territorial militiamen overtook these Indians and killed and wounded one, capturing the stolen horses and the meal and three of the Indian guns, but retreated when nine of their own number were wounded," the report added.

The attack great caused consternation in Sevier county and the angry settlers looked to Samuel Wear for leadership in taking effective action against the Indians, who were responsible for the deaths of a number of settlers in the region. A federal government order prohibited the use of volunteers for security operations on the frontier, but Samuel Wear ignored this in leading a party of volunteers in pursuit of the Indians. At Tallassee they killed 15 Indian men and one woman and took prisoner four women, who were later exchanged for the property stolen.

The incident was reported to the then secretary of state for war, but Tennessee Governor William Blount succeeded in having the affair glossed over. Blount approved the necessary military action to repel the attacks.

Samuel Wear was Sevier county's most prominent early settler, owning hundreds of acres of land. He served as county clerk for 27 years, under three separate governments: the state of Franklin, the Southwest Territory and the state of Tennessee and commanded troops in the War of 1812-14, alongside General Andrew Jackson.

Wear's first wife was Co Antrim-born Mary Thompson, the daughter of Elizabeth Lyle and James Thompson and the grand-daughter of Matthew Lyle, originally of Raloo near Larne, who settled in Rockbridge county, Virginia in 1740 and was a leading member of the Timber Ridge Presbyterian Church at Lexington.

Mary married Samuel Wear in Augusta county in 1778 when she was 21 and they had six children before her death in 1797. Wear's second wife was Mary Gilliland (she was 20 when they married in 1799) and she also bore him six children. Samuel Wear died in 1817 on his Sevierville plantation.

The mortise-tenon type home built by Samuel Wear at Pigeon Forge was not the typical Scots-Irish construction generally found in the Appalachian 18th century frontier region. The construction method was an arduous process, from the initial felling of the large logs to the roof erection.

The logs had to be shaped with the broad axe, each side cut and pointed from one end to another then turned until all four sides were shaped properly. After the square timber was formed an adze (a hoe-shaped axe) was used to put a smooth finish on the hewn wood. Timbers were then laid side by side to form a sound structural frame.

A one-room log house needed eight posts; three across the front wall; three across the back and two at the front corner of the chimney. At the foot of each post the wood was cut away to leave a tenon which would fit into a mortise in the sill. Each wall was fitted and pinned on the ground and then raised and pinned together to form a free-standing structure.

Planks for the floor and walls had to be sawed, and with no sawmills in the area the pioneers had to dig huge pits and work with a long pitsaw set in a frame. Each piece of wood was sawed by two men, one standing in the pit and the other on the timber above.

The Wear house was a two-storey building with a front porch which crossed the entire north side of the house. Stairs from the front porch led to the second storey where there were two large bedrooms, and the porch overlooked the Little Pigeon River which served for many years as the main way of travel to the Wear farm.

Samuel Wear is buried in the family cemetery adjoining the house, which was lived in until the 1950s when it was abandoned and fell into a state of disrepair.

THE WHITES

The family of John White was among the first to settle in "The Forks" section of North Carolina in what today is East Tennessee. John emigrated from Ireland to Pennsylvania and after passing through Virginia settled on 155 acres at Washington county. The family were leading members of New Bethel Presbyterian Church, founded by the Rev Samuel Doak, and James's gravestone is the second oldest in the church cemetery. He died in 1796. A son, Adam, was an elder in the church.

James White, very probably a kinsman of John White, was a revolutionary war hero who founded the city of Knoxville in 1791. White's grandfather Moses White and his wife Mary Campbell came originally from Argyllshire in Scotland and moved to Londonderry in the latter part of the 17th century.

His son Moses White 11 emigrated to Pennsylvania in 1741 and lived in Rowan county, North Carolina. James White was a renowned Indian fight in the Holston River settlements and his fort near Knoxville came under constant Cherokee Indian attack.

During the Revolutionary War, James White was a North Carolina militia captain and this entitled him to a land grant in the military reservation of the Cumberland River basin.

In October, 1791 he was given the task of laying out Knoxville as a proper settlement and, with three other Ulster-Scots the Rev Samuel Carrick, John Adair and George McNutt, he founded First Knoxville Presbyterian Church.

James White, as a politician, served as speaker in the general assembly of the lost state of Franklin which met in Jonesboro, now a part of East Tennessee. He was also a member of the territorial House of Representatives in Tennessee and served several terms as state senator and speaker.

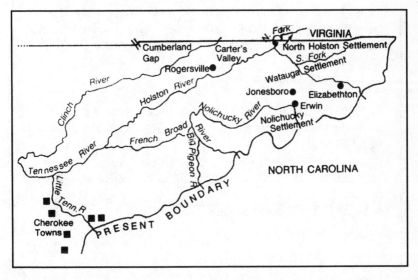

The early Scots-Irish settlements of East Tennessee (1770s-1780s)

The Boys from North Carolina

Some say it comes a-rollin' down the hollers of old Ireland,
And up the mountains of East Tennessee from back in North
  Carolina,
With Scottish tones and Indian moans and wails of railroad liners,
They helped along that old-tyme song, the boys from North
  Carolina.

It rolled and growed all in the West out in old Missouri,
And then took off around the world like lightning in its fury,
There ain't no way you sound the string in major or in minor,
It disappears all in the years and brings a laugh throughout the tears,
From the boys from North Carolina.

Kentucky is the Bluegrass state her sunny skies define her,
The western slope of East Tennessee there nothing could be finer,
The northern boys who make more noise to pick could not be finer,
To make that sound and get it down, it helps if you have been
  around,
The boys from North Carolina.

They stood in line around the block right back her at the Ryman,
To hear that lick, that old mule's kick from the boys from North
  Carolina,
Gastonia to Boiling Springs, from Flint Hill to Charlotte,
They tried to find the place of birth, still talking about who played
  it first,
Of the Boys from North Carolina.

                              JOHN HARTFORD MUSIC (BMI).

15

Curing illnesses *on the frontier*

The perennial tasks of healing the sick forced the 18th and 19th century frontier settlers of the Appalachian region to develop their own forms of cure. The herbs and plant life from the natural habitat of the mountains and forest were used to good effect by the medicine men who faithfully and lovingly tended to the people most in need.

The illnesses that were picked up living in the Appalachian back-country were not peculiar to one ethnic community - Scots-Irish, English or German. Although, sadly, the native American tribes like the Cherokees found that their immune systems were not sufficient to ward off diseases like smallpox and influenza which the white settlers were generally able to successfully counter.

It was said that a bout of smallpox brought from a slave ship anchored at Charleston in the early 18th century wiped out nearly half of the Cherokee nation. The Indian tribes relied on the extremely primitive and ineffective methods of their medicine men, who, obsessed with the perception of evil spirits, peddled in rattles, conjuring stones and various herbs and tree barks.

The various tribes put considerable store on the medicinal benefits of herbs, but many of these herbal remedies were later found to be scientifically unsound.

Smallpox was a terrible curse, even for afflicted whites, with the question of inoculation strenuously debated. Quarantine was essential for patients because those inoculated (by puncture in the arms) usually contracted a relatively mild case of the disease, but could pass on a more virulent form to those who had not been previously exposed.

The early frontier doctor had to be both a physician and nurse and, while he cured little in days when medical science was not so advanced, he generally managed to temporarily relieve the suffering and pain. Whisky was used as an anaesthetic and, when available, laudanum (an opium-based sedative) was a recommended pain-killer.

The doctor's duties extended to delivering babies, setting bones, opening boils, sewing up cuts and amputating limbs when it became a matter of life or death for the patient. From the first 18th century American frontier settlements, the doctor, like the clergyman and teacher, was a person the small isolated township communities looked up to and trusted, and many physicians travelled hundreds of miles on horseback to tend to the sick and infirmed.

In most cases, the doctor received no cash payment for his services and he was obliged to take whatever a family could offer - chickens or fish, bearskins, crafted materials and home-made tools. Very often, people tried their own medical remedies, by heating herbal doses over the hearth or consuming liquids that helped remove the pain.

Next to smallpox, tuberculosis was the most feared illness on the early western frontier with doctors baffled on how to treat a patient stricken with the disease. Other common diseases were typhoid fever, pneumonia, diphtheria, scarlet fever, rheumatism, diarrhoea and scurvy, but illness was also brought on by exposure in the cold winters and lack of proper food.

In some parts of Appalachia, however, the climate was looked upon as the physician. This was certainly the case in parts of East Tennessee and North Carolina hemmed in by the Allegheny and Cumberland mountains and enjoying the currents from the hot lowlands of the Carolinas and the Mississippi Valley.

It was said that so healthy were the inhabitants of this region, that from the first settlement of the territory in the 1760s until 1788, not a single trained doctor had settled there. This citation of "a clean bill of health" may have been a gross exaggeration, because proper medical records were not kept. The inaccessibility of the mountainous region was very probably a main reason why trained doctors were not established there.

However, one intrepid settler of the period was moved to write: "Our physicians are a fine climate; healthy, robust mothers and fathers; a plain and plentiful diet, and enough exercise. There is not a regularly bred physician in the whole district."

Herb doctors, who sought to cure diseases that the normal doctors could cure, were to be found in most back country communities and their methods, while not ethically approved in a physician's textbook, did find an approving public who felt the need to try unorthodox means of healing the sick, if the more conventional methods failed. Up until the turn of this century, a doctor's first task in treating a sick patient was to check the pulse and examine the tongue. With many battles and skirmishes fought along the frontier for a century and a half, the terrible wounds inflicted on unfortunate victims did stretch many doctors and nurses to breaking point.

Horrific injuries sustained in the Revolutionary War and, almost one hundred years later in the American Civil War, literally overwhelmed the medical and nursing profession of the times. The rapid advance of gangrene proved fatal for many horribly struck down by bullet, shell and mortar on the battlefield, or by arrow or tomahawk in Indian attacks. There were limits to what doctors could do then to save the lives of those afflicted by injuries or serious illness.

Many of the 18th century and early 19th century American settlers lived to a ripe old age, well beyond the accepted three score years and ten, but infant mortality was very common and it was not unusual for parents to lose as many as four or five children at birth or in early infancy.

This may have been one reason why frontier families ran into double figures and, very often, the health of the young mother - some married as young as fourteen and fifteen - suffered as a result and many died in their twenties and thirties.

With few if any hospitals or health clinics and laboratories in the backwood regions, the tasks of delivering babies and repairing broken limbs were highly delicate and dangerous. Doctors and nurses with the proper qualifications were in some mountainous localities a rarity and, in cases of childbirth, families had to improvise as best they could.

The "saddlebag doctors" travelled long distances on horseback to treat a patient and they had to rely on the contents of their saddlebags to effect a cure. The cures included flaxseed, red pepper, mustard poultices and herb teas. Many of these "doctors" had very little training in the grounding of medicines and any knowledge they had was picked up watching others putting into practice the healing methods of folk tradition.

This was a period when only the fittest survived and it was generally accepted that if a child held on to adulthood, his or her chances of long life were considerably enhanced. Records show that many Ulster men and women who had endured the rough passage across the Atlantic and moved over a period of forty and fifty years from the eastern seaboard areas through the various Appalachian states to the outer frontier lived until they were eighty or ninety. A few even reached the hundred-year mark.

With no proper hospitals and clinics, illness was a thing to be avoided at all costs by the settler families. If taken ill, their lives totally depended on whether their constitutions could overcome not just the disease, but the various improvised medicines used as a cure.

Some of the medicines used by the old-tyme physicians and, passed down from one generation to another, were peculiar to the landscape and the folk traditions of the Appalachian region:

- Lemon Balm - for coughs and colds
- Mint or Pennroyal - for colic in adults
- Catnip - for colic in babies
- Celandine - for warts
- Blackberry bark and root - for diarrhoea
- Pumpkin seeds - for tape worm
- Oil of cloves and oil of peppermint - for toothache
- Powdered rhubarb and oil of peppermint - for heartburn
- Tinc of aconite - for pleurisy
- Iodide of ammonium, spirit of chloroform and syrup senega - for pneumonia
- Dover powder - for convulsion
- Hysocine - for whooping cough and asthma
- Dover powder - for convulsion
- Sodium bromide and tinc foxglove - for palpitation
- Dover powder, Camphor and extract of Belladena - for influenza
  Note: More than sixty of the herbs used to cure sickness on the early Appalachian frontier are now listed in the modern America pharmacopoeia.

16

Ulster-Scots *on the Mississippi*

The Natchez territory of Mississippi was settled by Scots-Irish and Scottish highland settlers from 1763 and on hilly poor farmland they became "a border people" living on the highly dangerous edge of civilisation alongside Choctaw Indian reservations. During the early part of the 18th century French settlers controlled the Natchez lands, but there was a lot of blood-letting between the French and the local Indian tribes, centering around the 1729 massacre of Fort Rosalie (now Natchez).

For several decades between the French-Indian War and the start of the Revolutionary War in 1776 the British were in charge, and then, for a period, the Spanish had control until the American federalists got a foothold and seized the land in 1798. The white population of Natchez by this time was around 5,000.

Mississippi became a state of the Union on December 10, 1817 and Jefferson and Franklin counties covered the Natchez Scots-Irish settlements.

The Scots-Irish acted as a buffer to the Choctaw and Chickasaw Indians along the banks of the Mississippi and their townships were known as the "Scotch Settlements". These were expanded in 1780 when Miro, the Spanish governor, encouraged a number of Scots-Irish families to move from Kentucky and Tennessee. The settlements continued until about 1820.

There were several different routes that the early pioneers used to move their families to the Natchez territory. Many left the Pee Dee River area of South Carolina-North Carolina and travelled 200 miles along the Warriors Path to the Holston River in north-east Tennessee.

At Wilderness Road Fort near Kingsport, they built sturdy and spacious flat boats and used these to ferry the women, children, animal stock and food and personal and household items. One end of a flat boat was enclosed to provide protection from the elements; in effect, they were basic floating homes.

From the Holston the families moved along the Tennessee River, which they entered near Knoxville; reached the Ohio River at Paducah in Kentucky and on the last leg of the journey entered the Mississippi near Cairo, Illinois, before making the downward descent to Natchez. Indian attacks on the flat boat flotilla were a frequent occurrence and the settlers had always to be prepared, with the women steering the boats and the men engaging in battle. The perilous journey by water covered approximately 1,400 miles, with additional land distance of 300 miles.

Another route of migration was to travel by ship from the south east coast to Mobile, Alabama; overland to Lake Ponchatrain and flat boats and canoes took the families into south-west Mississippi. Some even took the more expensive and comfortable trip from the east coast to New Orleans by ship and they reached the Mississippi and Natchez on river boats.

Early records show that the settlers grew tobacco and indigo for shipment from Natchez to New Orleans and then to Cuba and Spain. The records also confirmed that some Presbyterian and Methodist church services were conducted in the Scottish Gallic language until after the Civil War, and the Psalms and the Shorter Catechism were written in the old dialect.

When the hostilities ended and treaties were drawn up, the Choctaw and Chickasaw tribes were moved into Oklahoma as part of President Andrew Jackson's ill-fated "Trail of Tears" in the 1830s. Much of their lands was taken over by some of the Scots-Irish families.

The Old Scotch settlement at Union and Ebenezer Presbyterian churches at the eastern end of Jefferson county was a mixture of Ulster-Scots and Scottish highlanders who had moved via North Carolina and Tennessee. The first settlers here in 1805 were George Torrey, his son Dongold; Laughlin Currie and Robert Willis. They were soon followed by the Gilchrists, Galbreaths and Camerons.

These families were noted for the simplicity of their manners; they were not wealthy, but plain, unpretending, honest God-fearing people. The history of the settlement is mainly a history of the two churches, organised soon after the arrival of the first families and through Presbyterian, and, indeed, Methodist influence the region became a prosperous and highly civilised area. The countryside was rich in game and the rivers in fish, and the land was extremely fertile for farming, with the hills and lowlands covered in canebrake. The settlers used the traditional Indian method of burning away the brake and planting the corn.

Some of the Scots-Irish were not averse to strong drink and an over-indulgence of whisky brought stern rebuke from elders in the church, even excommunication for a while. Records of Union and Ebenezer churches confirm firm dealings of the elders with their brethren: "Let a man be overtaken in a fault, such as violating the Sabbath day, or taking God's name in vain, or becoming intoxicated, and he was certain of discipline by the church."

The Dragoons militia company from Jefferson county, Mississippi, comprising many Scots-Irish lads, won distinction in the New Orleans campaign of 1813-1815, by routing a British division. This brought a glowing commendation from General Andrew Jackson, who said: "You have been the astonishment of one army, the admiration of another."

The Culbertsons, the Bradys and the Stephensons were among scores of Ulster Presbyterian families who migrated from Kentucky to the Natchez region of Mississippi. The Bradys were in Pennsylvania from the 1720s and later in the Carolinas, while the Culbertsons settled the New River area of Virginia before moving on to Chester county in South Carolina in the 1760s. All three families became connected through marriage.

The Culbertsons originally came from Ballygan near Ballymoney in Co Antrim and in 1730 three brothers - Alexander, Joseph and Samuel - emigrated to Lancaster county, Pennsylvania. They settled in Lurgan, Franklin county, Pennsylvania, and called their settlement "Culbertson's Row", after the home of their ancestors in Ulster. The family spread out after moving down the Great Wagon Road to South Carolina during the mid-1750s and Culbertsons were located in Kentucky, Tennessee, Georgia and Mississippi.

Josiah Culbertson served as major and Samuel Culbertson as a lieutenant and captain at the Battle of Kings Mountain and Cowpens. Robert and Joseph Culbertson were also listed at Kings Mountain, and engaged in various Indian wars.

The Stephensons from North Antrim came to America in 1772 with the fiercely independent Covenanting cleric the Rev William Martin, from Ballymoney. Records show that Alexander Brady married Elizabeth Stephenson in Chester county, South Carolina about 1775.

Many of the Bradys in the south eastern states were descended from the family of Hugh and Hannah Brady, who emigrated with their seven sons and two daughters from Enniskillen in Ulster to Lancaster, Pennsylvania between 1725 and 1730. The second son Captain John Brady and his son James were killed in western Pennsylvania in 1779 by a raising party led by Indian chief Bald Eagle. John's other son Samuel avenged the act by killing and scalping Bald Eagle.

Captain John Brady had an older brother Samuel, who was also a noted Indian fighter. He was one of two men who escaped from Fort Freeland in Pennsylvania at the time of its capture by Indians. He spent more than 30 years defending the Pennsylvanian borders, before moving to Indiana, where he died in 1811.

Controversy arose due to claims that the revenge act came after the armistice between the warring factions and Samuel Brady was tried and freed on condition that he leave the then United States. At this point, some of the Bradys moved into Kentucky and the North-West territory (Ohio), eventually making it to the Natchez region.

Captain John Brady was a distinguished soldier from the French-Indian War of 1754-63, serving in the Second Pennsylvanian regiment. He owned large tracts of land in the West Branch Valley of the Susquehanna River in Pennsylvania and he became a surveyor of land in the region.

In the years leading up to the Revolutionary War, John Brady went on several militia expeditions to Wyoming Valley and in the War he fought with General George Washington at Brandywine. A granite marker on John's grave bears the inscription: "Captain John Brady, fell in defense of our forefathers at Wolf Run. April, 11, 1779. Age 46 years."

John Brady and his wife Mary Quigley had 13 children, most of whom distinguished themselves in soldier, public office and in the Presbyterian Church.

William Robert Brady, another son of Hugh and Hannah, settled in Mecklenberg county, North Carolina about 1760. He had three sons Nathan, Joseph, and Alexander and their families are believed to have scattered to Georgia, Louisiana and south west Mississippi.

* The Natchez Trace was a trade route which extended from Natchez in Mississippi to Nashville in Tennessee. Indian tribes first developed the route, but it did not grow in commercial and military importance until the late 18th century. Boatmen once floated their goods down the Mississippi River to markets in Natchez and New Orleans and then travelled home along the Trace on foot.

In 1800 the Natchez Trace was made into a post road and during the war of 1812, General Andrew Jackson headed soldiers along the Trace to New Orleans and later used it during the Indian campaigns. The Trace was largely abandoned with the advent of the steamboat in the 1840s.

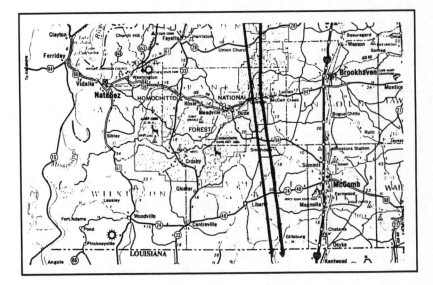

The Natchez region of Mississippi.

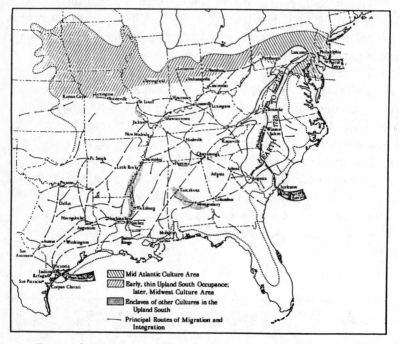

Extent of Mid-Atlantic culture in United States at initial occupance.

17

The Barbers *of County Antrim and Rocky Creek*

John Barber was a typical Ulster Presbyterian emigrant who moved to South Carolina in 1772 in the group led by Co Antrim Convenanting minister the Rev William Martin. Five ships were chartered in Belfast for that epic voyage to Charleston and Barber came across with relatives on the Pennsylvania Farmer.

As early as 1731, the colonial authorities of South Carolina were making attractive offers of land to what were termed "poor Protestants" from Ulster to settle in the up-country (Piedmont) territories of the state and when the William Martin group arrived the allocation to each "head of household" was 100 acres.

Under the terms of the state grants, the settlers were guaranteed security in their lands and possessions and the right to worship in the churches of their choice.

John Barber's 100 acres, his first property on American soil, was at Rocky Creek in Chester county, where the Rev William Martin established his inter-denominational church which he called "Catholic". Over the next three decades, the Barber lands were extended into the adjoining York county and, through the Revolutionary War period, he served in the South Carolina state militia.

Barber is recorded in the Revolutionary War index as having rented wagons to the army and he also collaborated in providing provisions to the troops with a Mary Barber, believed to be his sister. One such sale was 250lbs of beef for South Carolina state troops in 1782 which fetched three pounds, four shillings and twopence sterling. Good value for beef even in those days!

Other Barber family members who travelled from Belfast to Charleston in 1772 were James, who joined John on the Pennsylvania Farmer, and Samuel, Isabel, James and Joseph, who arrived on the ship Lord Dunluce. Like John, they all received South Carolina land entitlements in Chester county.

John Barber's wife was Mary Agnew, who had moved from Belfast in 1772 with her family as a five-year-old on board the Lord Dunluce. When they married, there were 19 years between John and 16-year-old Mary, a common enough thing on the American frontier when young women were wed in their early teens. They had eight children, five sons and three daughters.

John Barber died in 1843, aged 95, predeceasing his wife Mary by 23 years. They are buried in the cemetery of Beersheba Presbyterian Church in York county, one of the oldest Presbyterian meeting houses in the Carolina Piedmont.

Logo of South Carolina.

18

Ulstermen who made it
to the White House

Thirteen of the 41 Presidents of the United States have direct families links to the north of Ireland and the Scots-Irish immigrants who moved to America in the 18th century and early 19th century. Three of these Presidents also served as Vice-Presidents, with a fourth John C. Calhoun occupying the No 2 position in the White House for two terms.

UNITED STATES PRESIDENTS:

- **Andrew Jackson (1829-37).** Democrat. Co Antrim stock.
- **James Knox Polk (1845-49).** Democrat. Co Londonderry/Co Donegal stock.
- **James Buchanan (1857-61).** Democrat. Co Donegal stock.
- **Andrew Johnson (1865-69).** Democrat. Co Antrim stock.
- **Ulysses Simpson Grant (1869-1877).** Republican. Co Tyrone stock.
- **Chester Alan Arthur (1881-85).** Republican. Co Antrim stock.
- **Grover Cleveland (1885-89 and 1893-97).** Democrat. Co Antrim stock.
- **Benjamin Harrison (1889-93).** Republican. Co Antrim stock.
- **William McKinley (1897-1901).** Republican. Co Antrim.
- **Woodrow Wilson (1913-21).** Democrat. Co Tyrone stock.
- **Richard Millhouse Nixon (1969-74).** Republican. Co Antrim stock
- **James Earl Carter (1976-81).** Democrat. Co Antrim stock
- **William Jefferson Clinton (1993-).** Democrat. Co Fermanagh stock

Six of these Presidents were Presbyterians (Jackson, Polk, Buchanan, Cleveland, Harrison and Wilson), three were Methodists (Johnson, Grant and McKinley), with two Baptists (Carter and Clinton), one Episcopalian (Arthur) and one Quaker (Nixon). Three - Jackson, Buchanan and Johnson - were born in log cabins, with Jackson's birth in March, 1767 recorded only 18 months after his parents moved from Ulster.

The wives of Andrew Jackson and Andrew Johnson - Rachel Donelson Jackson and Eliza M. McCardle - were both second generation Ulster-Scots, while bachelor James Buchanan's first lady in the White House was his niece Harriet Lane. Rachel Donelson was a member of a Co. Antrim family, while Eliza Johnson was of Co. Tyrone stock.

UNITED STATES VICE-PRESIDENTS:

- **John C. Calhoun (1825-32).** Democrat. Co Donegal/Co Londonderry stock.
- **Andrew Johnson (1865).** Democrat. Co Antrim stock.
- **Chester Alan Arthur (1881).** Republican. Co Antrim stock.
- **Richard Millhouse Nixon (1953-1961).** Republican. Co Antrim stock

Andrew Johnson became President on the assassination of President Abraham Lincoln in 1865.

Chester Alan Arthur became President on the assassination of President James A. Garfield in 1881.

President William McKinley was assassinated in 1901.

19

The final hours *of Andrew Jackson*

President Andrew Jackson may not have been especially religious during the greater part of his life and until his last few years he was not a regular attender of church. But Jackson was certainly not the heathen some churchmen of the period believed him to be and he never forgot the fundamentals of the faith his mother Elizabeth taught him as a child.

Jackson's personal attachment to Christianity was experienced by Tennessee Presbyterian cleric the Rev James Gallagher during a pastoral visit to the ageing President at his Hermitage home outside Nashville in 1843.

The Rev Gallagher recalled: "The old hero was then very frail and had the appearance of extreme old age; but he was reposing with calmness and confidence on the promise and covenant of God. He had been a member of the church for several years."

During the conversation which took place, Andrew Jackson turned to Mr Gallagher and remarked: "There is a beautiful hymn on the subject of the exceeding great and precious promise of God to His people. It was the favourite hymn of my wife Rachel, till the day of her death. It commences in this way: 'How firm a foundation, ye saints of the Lord.' I wish you would sing it now."

So the little company sang the entire hymn:

"How firm a foundation, ye saints of the Lord,
Is laid for your faith in His excellent word!
What more can He say than to you He has said,
You, unto Jesus for refuge have fled?

"In every condition - in sickness, in health,
In poverty's vale, or abounding in wealth;
At home or abroad, on the land, on the sea,
As days may demand, shall thy strength ever be.

"Fear not, I am with thee, O be not dismayed!
I, I am thy God, and will still give thee aid;
I'll strengthen thee, help thee, and cause thee to stand,
Upheld by My righteous omnipotent hand.

"When through the deep waters I cause thee to go,
The rivers of woe shall not thee overflow;
For I will be with thee, thy troubles to bless,
And sanctify to thee thy deepest distress.

"When through fiery trails thy pathway shall lie,
My grace all-sufficient shall be thy supply;
The flame shall not hurt thee; I only design,
Thy dross to consume, and thy gold to refine.

"The soul that on Jesus has leaned for repose,
I will not, I will not desert to its foes;
That soul, through all hell should endeavour to shake,
I'll never, no never, no never forsake."

Andrew Jackson - he served two Presidential terms from 1828 to
1836 - was born a Presbyterian of God-fearing Ulster parents from
Boneybefore near Carrickfergus in Co Antrim who wanted him to
become a Presbyterian minister.

Jackson endeavoured to live by the sound advice his mother
Elizabeth gave him when he saw her for the last time in 1780 when she
headed to Charleston to nurse revolutionary soldiers imprisoned by the
British. She died in Charleston, but her parting words to Andrew were:
"Make friends by being honest, keep them by being steadfast; Andy .
. . never tell a lie, nor take what is not your own, nor sue . . . for
slander . . . settle them cases yourself."

Although he took a very secular approach for most of his life and
delayed formally joining a church until after he had retired to his

Hermitage home in Tennessee, Jackson enjoyed reading the Bible and considered himself a practising Christian. Another favourite book of his was the Oliver Goldsmith classic The Vicar of Wakefield.

An assassination bid was made on Andrew Jackson in the retunda of the Capitol building in Washington on January 30, 1835. The shots, fired from only a few feet away, narrowly missed the President and a man was quickly arrested and later declared insane.

Jackson's wife Rachel was a strongly evangelical Presbyterian, but he did not become an official church member until 1738. He said the reason he refused to join the church was that it would be looked upon as a political act if he did.

As a child growing up the Waxhaws region of the Carolinas in the 1770s he had, of course, learned the basics of religion and studied under the tuition of Dr William Humphries and the Rev James White Stephenson.

Andrew Jackson died of chronic tuberculosis on June 8, 1845, aged 78. His dying wish was that he would meet all his friends on the other side - "both white and black" - he emphasised. His last words were "Oh, do not cry. Be good children, and we shall all meet in heaven." The old man was buried in a simple ceremony next to his wife Rachel in The Hermitage grounds.

Rachel Jackson, the daughter of Colonel John Donelson whose family originated from East Co Antrim, was said to be the type of Tennessee frontierswoman whose culture and refinement influenced the times. Jackson's attachment to her during the years of their marriage never waned and when she died in 1828, aged sixty-one, he was inconsolable.

"No political burden ever bore down upon him as did the loss of his companion. His love for her during life and his increasing devotion to her memory are tributes to the strength and amiability of her character," wrote Tennessee historian Oliver Taylor.

President Jackson was deeply conscious of the cultural differences that permeated the American regions in the early 19th century. In his farewell address to the nation, he said: "In a country so extensive as the United States and, with pursuits so varied, the internal regulations of the various states must frequently differ from one another in important particulars; and this difference is unavoidably increased by the varying principles upon which the American colonies were originally planted; principles which had taken root in their social relations before the Revolution, and, therefore, of necessity influencing their policy since they became free and independent states. But each state has an unquestionable right to regulate its own internal concerns."

SCHISMS THAT DISRUPTED THE UNION

John C. Calhoun, the son of a Co Donegal Presbyterian, used his last address to the United States Senate in 1850 to bemoan the major schisms that had developed in the Presbyterian, Methodist and Baptist churches in America as a prelude to the break-up of the American nation in the Civil War of 1861-65.

"It is a great mistake to suppose that disunion can be effected by a single blow," he warned. "The cords which bound these states together in one common Union are far too numerous and powerful for that," said Calhoun.

The distinguished South Carolina senator traced the process whereby the three great Protestant evangelical denominations had created ecclesiastical communities that in the early Antebellum period in America "embraced the whole Union." Principal laymen and clerics of each denomination, he said, had met annually to transact business relating to their common concerns.

"They devised plans for disseminating the Bible, establishing missions, distributing tracts and establishing presses for the publication of tracts, newspapers and periodicals, with a view to diffusing religious information for the support of their respective doctrines and creeds. Taken as a whole those efforts contributed greatly to strengthen the bonds of the Union. The ties which held each denomination together formed a strong cord to hold the Union together."

Regrettably, the North and the South divided in four years of bloody conflict and the denominational bonds that united Presbyterians, Methodists and Baptists snapped under the strain of the intense and, in some places, explosive debate on slavery.

John C. Calhoun's comments should be put against the context of the Scots-Irish commitment to their Calvinist faith. Many of the early 18th century Presbyterian settlers saw themselves as a people who came to America because they saw no prospect in the future that they would be permitted to enjoy modes of worship which they believed were most in accordance with God's word.

In Appalachian pioneering communities, the various churches - Presbyterian, Methodist, and Baptist - exerted a strong moral influence on their people. The Presbyterian Church, in particular, with its orderly form of government, supervised regularly on disciplinary cases, with procedures set forth, citations issued and witnesses called before adjudication was decided upon.

Very often, the church session served in the place of civil courts for congregational members and cases were sometimes referred to the Presbytery for final judgment. The trials were concerned with fraud in business dealings, brawling, drunkenness, break-up in marital relationships, sexual impropriety, as well as absence from church and Sabbath-breaking.

The punishment for the offender was either a monetary fine or the withdrawal for a period of church privileges. The latter sentence the more severe in communities who lived by Old Testament principles.

The Presbyterian Church of the 18th century demanded of its members scrupulous knowledge of the Bible and the catechisms and regular attendance at worship. The Presbyterian frontier settlers may not have been always pious and zealous, but the church was their first badge of identity with the other ethnic groups, proclaiming a proud heritage from days when their ancestors resisted the diktats of kings and ecclesiastical oppressors.

Sunday was a day of strict observance on the American frontier. All work ceased, with the whole day given over to religion. In the Shenandoah Valley historians record that Sunday services continued from 10 am until sunset, with an hour set aside for dinner.

In Presbyterian tradition, the expounding of the Word from the Bible was the central part of the service.

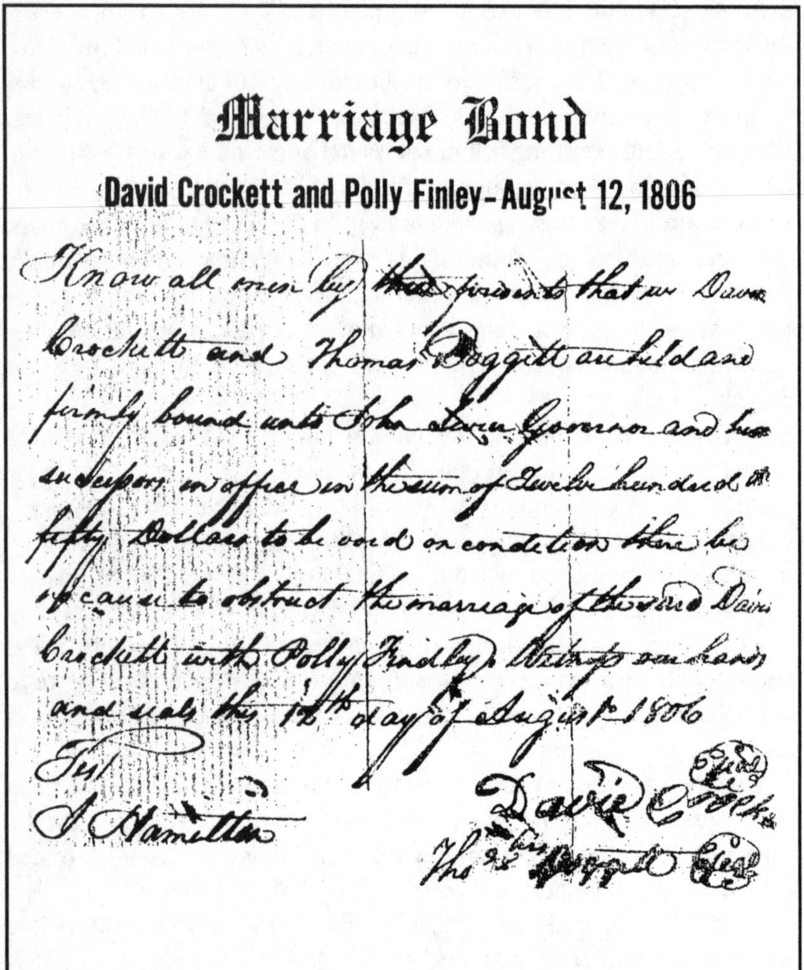

Marriage Bond

David Crockett and Polly Finley–August 12, 1806

Know all men by these presents that we David Crockett and Thomas Doggett are held and firmly bound unto John Sevier Governor and his successors in office in the sum of twelve hundred and fifty Dollars to be void on condition there be no cause to obstruct the marriage of the said David Crockett with Polly Findley. Witness our hands and seals this 12th day of August 1806

Test

J. Hamilton

David Crockett (seal)

Thos. his Doggett (seal)

Marriage bond of David Crockett and Polly Finley.

20

Davy Crockett - *man with a vision and an ideal in life*

Few American frontiersmen were as extraordinary, as exceptional or as inspiring as Davy Crockett, the "king of the wild frontier" whose great grandfather William left the north west part of Ulster for the "New World" in the early part of the 18th century.

Crockett, a humble straight-talking man who preferred to be called David rather than Davy, personified the finest qualities of the Scots-Irish pioneers in a much too short 49-year lifetime. He left an indelible mark on the rugged landscapes of his Tennessee homeland and the stories of his exploits and achievements will always be a cornerstone of American folklore.

David's days ended in Texas in March, 1836 - in tragic circumstances at Fort Alamo, but his heart was always embedded in the rich soil of the Tennessee hills and hollows and there was hardly an acre in the picturesque Volunteer state that he did not frequent at some time during his life.

In fact, David resided in at least seven different locations in Tennessee. He lived the first twenty five years in East Tennessee; the next ten in Middle Tennessee and the last fourteen, all but a few months when he went on the call of duty to Texas, in the wild sparsely inhabited West Tennessee.

David was the fifth son and ninth child of John and Rebecca Hawkins Crockett, born in a one-room cabin in a clearing just beside the Limestone River in Greene County, East Tennessee. The Crocketts

- from North Tyrone and East Donegal in Ulster - had reached Tennessee (then part of North Carolina) via Pennsylvania, Maryland and the Shenandoah Valley of Virginia.

Some historical records claim the family originated from 17th century French Huguenot stock (Crocketagne) and they reached Ireland by way of England and Scotland. Several family members were involved in defending Londonderry in the 1688-89 Siege and one of the first Crocketts to reach America in the early 18th century was Joseph Louis, who was married to Sarah Stewart, from Co Donegal.

Other branches of the Crockett family emigrated from Co Antrim in the 1730s and, after settlement in the Shenandoah Valley, settled in South and North Carolina, Tennessee and Missouri.

In November, 1777, David Crockett's grandparents were massacred in an Indian attack on their homestead at Carter's Valley in Hawkins county, near the present-day town of Rogersville. David's father John was not at home at the time, but his uncle James was taken captive and did not return for 20 years. The incident deeply scarred the family and their Scots-Irish kinsfolk in that part of East Tennessee.

From childhood, David Crockett was street wise in the ways of the rugged Tennessee countryside - roaming the forests and mountains, exploring new territory, hunting wild game and fishing in the great rivers that traversed the region. Roaming was a significant characteristic in his life and he was never one to settle in one place for any length of time. Sometimes as many as five or six localities or cabins or houses claimed him as an inhabitant; it was said "he knew the confines of no walls for a very long period of time."

David Crockett filled many roles: faithful husband to his first wife Polly Finley, and on her death to his second wife Elizabeth Patton; loving father to three children John Wesley, William and Margaret Polly; hunter, explorer and adventurer; soldier and politician; celebrated storyteller, folklorist and wit; certainly a man with the common touch, one who was fully aware of precisely where he had come from and where he was going.

Here was a man possessed with all the traits of the pioneering Scots-Irish: tough, determined, cantankerous, humourous, independent, thrifty and imbued with a large degree of plain common sense. David Crockett became an heroic figure to millions of Americans, during his lifetime and in the generations since. Behind the myth, we find a strong-willed, determined and unyielding personality.

Never a man of means, David Crockett's obvious lack of finance curtailed to a significant degree his political career and, although he served three terms in the United States Congress and stood on a platform that upheld real justice and democracy, he found it difficult to compete with opponents from the upper and merchant classes who could always find money when it came to buying votes.

Crockett's role as a legislator was commended even by his political opponents. David consistently spoke and acted on behalf of the economic, educational and social progress of his backwoods constituents, a high proportion of them Scots-Irish Presbyterian stock, and his moral courage and undying patriotism were a virtue. He had little formal education, but he was quick to learn and, on his own initiative, he acquired the essential knowledge to take a principled and honoured stand in the corridors of power.

James Wakefield Burke, in his book *David Crockett - the Man Behind the Myth*, wrote of the legendary Tennessean: "David Crockett, the son of a poor Scotch-Irish immigrant from Carolina, possessed the essential attributes for the West. He was an adventurer, with a talent for falling in with strangers, a memory for names and faces, a gift of storytelling, inexhaustible invention, an indomitable valiance, a remarkable ability for sharp-shooting, and that freedom from conscience that springs from a contempt for pettiness and bureaucracy.

"Crockett was a free soul and he sought only the company of men of like temperament. There seems to have been graven into this liber- ated man from the dirt farms of Tennessee a reluctance to be tied down, to be obligated for long to any engagement, to own anything save his long rifle."

David Crockett was indeed his own man, and although he had stood shoulder to shoulder with another famous Scots-Irishman General Andrew Jackson in various battles, he parted company when Jackson became President - over land and river issues that greatly affected the livelihoods of his people.

He said in March, 1830: "To General Jackson, I am a firm and undeviating friend. I have fought under his command . . . I have loved him . . . and still love him; but to be compelled to love every one who for . . . self aggrandizement pretend to rally around the 'Jackson Standard' is what I can never submit to. The people . . . ought to look out for breakers! The fox is about; let the roost be guarded."

Crockett and other Tennessean representatives were disappointed at Jackson's stand against financial aid for the improvement in the transportation facilities of the state. Crockett strongly believed in human rights, including those of the native American people, and he led opposition to Andrew Jackson's Indian policy of forcing the tribes living east of the Mississippi River to move to the western part of the Louisiana territory. When the bill approving the measure at a cost of 500,000 dollars was put before Congress in 1830, Crockett was the only Tennessean to vote against it.

His main objection was that he did not want to see "the poor remnants of a once powerful people" forced to move "against their will". David represented four counties in West Tennessee on the border of the Chickasaw country, and he was appalled at the decision to drive those Indians west of the Mississippi. He also knew that the many by now-peaceful Cherokees would prefer "death in their homes" to moving away from their natural environment in Tennessee.

During the passage of the Indian bill in Congress, Crockett said: "I am at liberty to vote as my conscience and judgment dictate to be right, without the yoke of any party on me, or the driver at my heels, with the whip in his hands, commanding me to 'gee-whoa-haw' just at his pleasure."

David Crockett also enjoyed the reputation of being "the champion" of the rights of occupants or squatters who had settled on land in West Tennessee before it had been legally acquired from the Indians and opened out to proper settlement

He deeply mistrusted the federal government over its legislation on the territorial state remits of Tennessee and North Carolina which dated back to the wrangling over the lost state of Franklin in the 1780s.

Crockett also irked the Washington establishment in 1830 when he put forward a resolution to abolish the nation's military academy at West Point. His main argument was that only the sons of the rich and influential could get into West Point, and that the bounty of the government should go to the poor rather than to the rich. He contended that the War of 1812 had shown that a man could fight the battles of his country and lead his country's armies, without being educated at West Point; as shown by the success of General Andrew Jackson, who had since progressed to the highest office in the land.

Although David Crockett was of a Scots-Irish Presbyterian family, he is not thought to have had close formal ties to particular churches in the Tennessee frontier regions where he lived. Very little is documented on David's religious leanings, but like others who roamed the wild and dangerous terrain of the American frontier country he would have felt the need to believe in the existence of a supreme being. Both his wives Polly Finley and Elizabeth Patton were from strong Scots-Irish Presbyterian families and religion would have been an important marker in their lives.

His parents John and Rebecca certainly were God-fearing folks, typical of the times, and when David was born, an elderly German midwife told his proud mother: "Ach, Rebecca, der Junger looks like a bright star - the star of David."

David was once financially aided by a generous benefactor when his money ran out during an election campaign, as it very often did, and he later repaid the gesture with the presentation to his helper of a Bible. David obviously appreciated the inspirational value of the good book!

Contemporaries of David Crockett wrote of him as "always a pleasant, courteous and interesting man" . . . "of fine instincts and intellect" . . . "a man with a high sense of honor, of good morals, not intemperate, nor a gambler."

After David Crockett's death at the Alamo in 1836, his son John Wesley represented West Tennessee in Congress for several years. He also died a young man, aged only 44.

A proud Tennessean's lament

"Farewell to the Mountains whose mazes to me
Were more beautiful far than Eden could be;
No fruit was forbidden, but Nature had spread
Her bountiful board, and her children were fed.
The hills were all garners - our herds wildly grew,

And nature was shepherd and husbandman too.
I felt like a monarch, yet thought like a man,
As I thanked the Great Giver and worshipped His plan.

"The home I foresake where my offspring arose;
The graves I forsake where my children repose.
The home I redeemed from the savage and wild:
The home I have loved as a father his child.
The corn that I planted, the fields that I cleared,
 The flocks that I raised, and the cabin I reared;
The wife of my bosom - Farewell to ye all!
In the land of the stranger I rise or I fall.

"Farewell to my country! - I fought for thee well,
When the savage rushed forth like the demons from hell.
In peace or in war I have stood by thy side,
My country for thee I have lived, would have died!
But I cast off - my career now is run
And I wonder abroad like the prodigal son,
Where the wild savage roves, and the broad prairies spread,
The fallen - despised - will again go ahead!"

These were the last verses of poetry written poignantly by frontiers-man and politician David Crockett in 1835 after he finished his final term in the United States Congress and before he left Tennessee for the Alamo in Texas where he was to die on March 6, 1836 at the hands of Mexican assailants.

Thirty-four Tennesseans died at the Alamo, including David Crockett, who said when he arrived to defend the besieged Tex-Mex border outpost: "I have come to aid you all that I can in your cause . . . and all the honor that I desire is that of defending as a high private . . . the liberties of our common country."

21

Tough Ulster stock *who braved danger in hostile Indian territory*

The earliest Presbyterian Church in Middle Tennessee was established by the Rev Thomas Craighead in 1785 at Fort Haysboro, situated between present-day Nashville and the town of Gallatin. The congregation comprised mostly of Scots-Irish settlers who had moved from the Shenandoah Valley and North Carolina into territory that was dangerous and wild, inhabited by hostile Cherokee and Shawnee Indian tribes, who deeply resented the white incursions on to their lands.

A number of pioneers buried in the Spring Hill cemetery of the Old Haysboro Meeting House lost their lives in bloody encounters with Indians. This area was the outer American frontier in the 1780s-1790s and only the hardiest and the most courageous of people would have ventured there. The grim catalogue of massacres of white settlers and retribution killings of Indian tribesmen terribly stained the region.

The Rev Thomas Craighead is buried in Spring Hill cemetery and also interred in a plot marked by a quaint old Gothic headstone is Co Antrim-born Margaret (Peggy) Brown, who was born in Ireland in 1701 and died in 1801, aged one hundred years, five months and seventeen days.

Margaret was a real pioneer, who, when she was 84, braved the perils with her family and in-laws over a journey of hundreds of miles over mountains and through dangerous Indian country from North Carolina to Haysboro.

Family records state that Peggy's father, Joseph Fleming, was a land owner of substance in Ulster and as a teenager she married William Brown, from Londonderry, where the couple lived for a number of years and where six of their seven children were born. Members of the Brown and Fleming families defended Londonderry for the Protestant Williamite cause in the Siege of 1688-89.

William Brown prospered in Londonderry as a farmer, but he had a hankering for more land and in 1745 he and his family sailed for America, landing at New Castle, Delaware. The Browns spent the next ten years living in Pennsylvania (Lancaster county) and the Shenandoah Valley of Virginia and, by May, 1747, they were on the move to Guilford county in North Carolina, to take up a land grant of 411 acres from the Earl of Granville, acting on behalf of King George 11.

The farm at North Buffalo Creek was a dream come true for William, but he did not live long to enjoy the newly-acquired land and died just before Christmas of 1757. He was 70, his wife 14 years younger. William's grave is not marked, but his son Joseph erected a monument in his memory at the Sally Reed burying ground at Anderson, South Carolina. Details of his death are recorded in the family Bible passed down through generations.

Colonel James Brown, the youngest son of William and Peggy, moved with his wife Jane Gillespie after the Revolutionary War from Guilford county in North Carolina to Maury county in Middle Tennessee. Colonel Brown had been given a certificate payable in western lands for his military service and the move was to have tragic consequences for the family in May, 1788.

Brown made a preliminary trip to the region to select a tract of land and, while he returned to round up the family for the journey to new territory, two of his sons Daniel and William were left to prepare a clearing and build a log cabin.

A large boat was built on the Holston River, and two-inch planks placed around the gunwales had holes for firing and the vessel was equipped with a small swivel gun to ward off hostile Indians in the dangerous river journey to Middle Tennessee.

The party that set off included James Brown; his wife Jane (Gillespie); four sons James, John, Joseph and George; three daughters Jane, Elizabeth and Polly; five other young men and a black woman.

Five days after leaving the Holston region, the Browns were "befriended" at the Tennessee River near Chattanooga by Indian chief Cotetoy and two of his tribesmen from the Tuskagee River township. Other Indians were alerted and 40 of them arrived in a fleet of canoes, hoisting a flag of truce. They indicated a desire to trade, but they had rifles under their blankets and James Brown allowed them to board his boat, with disastrous results.

In a bloody assault, James's head was cut from his body and thrown into the river.

Two of his sons James and John and the five young men who had joined the family were also killed in the massacre and the surviving members of the family - wife Jane and five children - were taken captive. One son was held by the Shawnees for five years and Jane Brown and one of her daughters were forced to march hundreds of miles to Ohio. They returned to settle in Maury county and the county's first court was held in the log cabin home of a son Joseph, one of those taken captive by the Indians.

Jane Gillespie Bown, whose Gillespie family had emigrated from Ulster at about the same time as the Browns, lived in Maury county until her death in 1831. On her tombstone in a disused cemetery off the main street in Columbia, the county capital, is an inscription relating the facts of the May, 1788 massacre and carrying the poignant footnote: "The reason I tell you these things O reader is so you will know at what cost this liberty which you enjoy today was won for you."

A few months before the Brown attack, three frontier surveyors Captain William Pruett, Moses Brown and Daniel Johnson were killed by Indians, and, in another incident, leading frontierman Colonel Anthony Bledsoe lost his life. These attacks were avenged by the local militia force, led by James Robertson, one of the heroes of the Battle of Kings Mountain, and the tension increased when Indian chief Big Foot was killed by William Pillow, a young man with close family connections to the Browns.

The Brown massacre and other Indian killings had a devastating effect on the Scots-Irish settlers and tensions remained high for several decades until peace treaties and population movement of the tribes brought the violent hostilities to an end.

Peggy Brown, the family matriarch, spent her latter days with her youngest daughter Jane, who married Reese Porter, the son of Ulster-born couple Hugh and Violet Mackey Porter. Hugh Porter was a justice of the peace at Orange county North Carolina and he owned 393 acres of land close to the Brown homestead in Guilford county. Reese, a formidable man six feet, six inches in height, served like his father in the militia and during the Revolutionary War he saw action at the Battle of Guilford Courthouse.

Family records claim Jane Porter stole through enemy lines during the War to free her husband, who was being held captive in a log cabin, and, significantly for his militia service, Reese received land grants of 3,640 acres at the Tennessee, Elk and Duck Rivers in Middle Tennessee.

The problem with this land was that Cherokee Indians still had the proper legal rights to it and, during the twenty years of a protracted wrangle, Reese and his family lived in the Nashville area. His wife Jane died just before they were given the go-ahead in 1806 to move on to the land and the Porter plantation, on Reese's death, extended to more than 2,500 acres.

Reese and Jane Porter had eight sons and the land in Middle Tennessee was divided out among them. Jane's brother Joseph married Mary Porter, Reese's sister.

Grandsons of William and Peggy Brown fought with General Andrew Jackson in the War of 1812: Lieutenant Colonel Joseph Brown commanding the 27th Infantry Regiment, serving alongside Lieutenant William Porter.

The Browns and the Porters, who were also connected through marriage with the Pillow and Sterrett families from Ulster, were strong Presbyterian stock, closely identified with the congregations in the various regions that they settled.

•••

President Theodore Roosevelt said the Scots-Irish "suffered terrible injuries at the hands of the Indian tribes, and on their foes they waged a terrible warfare in return." He observed, "They were relentless, revengeful, suspicious, knowing neither ruth nor pity. But they were also upright, resolute and fearless, loyal to their friends, and devoted to their country."

22

Frontier documents
properly signed and sealed

Wills and testaments were essential documents to be drawn up by Scots-Irish settlers on the American frontier where land and a person's material possessions were kept strictly within the confines of the family circle.

The extent of the detail in the 18th century wills, testaments and land sales is incredible for the period, with court seals appended and appropriate signatures added to the documents drawn up by county clerks and lawyers, who effectively shaped the mould of pioneering society.

Frontier land had been acquired in perilous life and death situations for the first settlers and nothing was left to chance by them or their descendants in the passing on of their holdings and personal chattels. Throughout the Appalachian states of the United States today land has been in the possession of many families since the first white settlements of up to ten generations ago, and, in most cases, it is not for sale, at any price.

Blood, sweat and tears was shed by the early pioneers to obtain the land in the dark, dangerous years of the 18th century and it was tradition in families to pass it on to their succeeding generations.

The Scots-Irish, being a community which totally assimilated into American life at the early stages of development, were largely instrumental in drawing up and administering the rules and legalities in many counties of Virginia, Tennessee, the Carolinas, Kentucky and Georgia.

They were certainly not a people to be caught out by competitors or predators from other ethnic communities like the English and Germans in the sale or lease of land. They could meticulously account for every square foot of farmland and every stick of furniture and valuable on their homesteads.

In his will of 1779, David Kinkead of Washington county, Virginia left to his wife Winnifred his five cows and young black horse, his beds and furniture; the best of the irons pots and the house Bible for the duration of her life, all to be passed on in time to her son Joseph.

The Kinkead plantation and plantation tools of every sort were left to his grandson David, on the understanding that he took care of and maintained his grandmother while she lived. Adjoining portions of land were allocated to other members of the family, with David's colt revolver and rifle being passed on to another grandson.

Money was rarely mentioned in wills, but it could be taken for granted that whatever liquid cash there was stayed put in the family coffers. Bartering for material goods, of course, was the accepted pattern of life 200-250 years ago and it was not always necessary to exchange amounts of money for goods purchased.

In those days land was measured literally from tree to tree, with the sale at Sullivan county, Tennessee in 1797 of 500 acres to George Rutledge by David Kinkead, executor of the estate of Joseph Kinkead (deceased) a classic example.

The sale stipulated "a certain tract of land containing five hundred acres in the county of Sullivan, beginning at three white oaks and a black oak thence north 60 degrees west along William Armstrong's line and seventy two poles to a hickory and pine, thence contiguous with said Armstrong's line north one hundred and thirty eight poles to a chestnut tree on Benjamin Looney's corner; then with this line north 55 degrees east ninety eight poles to a white oak on said Looney's corner, then with his line north forty six poles to a hickory, then north thirty degrees east seventy two poles to a white hickory, then south twenty four degrees east seventy eight poles to a black oak and hickory, then north seventy two degrees east two hundred and sixty four poles to the William Snodgrass line."

The Kinkead sale was signed by the Sullivan county clerk Mathew Rhea, a grandson of former Co Donegal Presbyterian minister the Rev

Joseph Rhea, who was an early pioneering pastor in East Tennessee. Matthew Rhea published in 1832 the first map of Tennessee, based on actual land surveys, a remarkable achievement considering the size and logistical shape of Tennessee.

The Kinkeads, of Co Antrim stock, and the Rutledges, from Co Tyrone, were prominent families in East Tennessee in the late 18th century.

Even back in Ulster during this period, a family will was very carefully drawn up. The will made in March, 1765 by farmer Samuel Mophet, of Ballylig near Broughshane in Rathcavin parish, Co Antrim, ensured that things were left right and proper for his departure from the scene of time.

"The last will and testament of Samuel Mophet, who being weak in body, but of perfect mind and memory, thanks be to God for all His mercies. Knowing it is appointed to all men to die, I commit my soul to God Who gave it, and my body to be buried in a decent Christian manner in Broughshane.

"I first leave and bequeath to my well-loved wife Martha McCulley and her son Thomas Mophet the equal third of my lease and holding at Ballylig during her life and in case she die, to fall to the said Thomas at her decease. I also leave to my son John, one-third of said holding, and to my son William one-third of all the implements to be kept for use of the said farm.

"I leave my sorrel horse to my son John, the black filly to my son William, and to my daughters Mary and Margaret I leave four head of cows each; and to my wife and daughter Margaret what sheep I as am possest, and leave the rest of my black cattle to my wife and son Thomas."

Presbyterian Covenanter William Mophet, his wife Barbara Chestnut and son Samuel sailed from Belfast to Charleston in South Carolina in August, 1772 on board the ship Mary Jane. They settled on 500 acres at Rocky Creek in the Carolina piedmont and William served as a militia man in the Revolutionary War.

Marriage bonds on the American frontier were usually drawn up with enough propriety and care to ensure that they were legally binding to the two parties. The marriage bond of legendary hunter, soldier and politician David Crockett and his first wife Polly Finley was properly signed and sealed in Jefferson county, Tennessee on August 12, 1806 after the marriage at the Finley home at Bay's Mountain.

The couple met at a "reaping" party in the spring of that year and, after David indicated that he wished to marry Polly, he contracted with the son of a Quaker friend John Cannaday to work six months for a horse with which to begin supporting his would-be family. David's marriage to Polly lasted until 1815, when she died leaving three small children - two sons and an infant daughter.

A typical East Tennessee will.

23

Shared farm methods *in the wilds of the frontier*

The Scots-Irish settlers may have endured many violent run-ins with the native American Indian tribes through the 18th century, but they shared a common currency in things like farming and reconnoitering the Appalachian mountains and forests to eke out a living.

Indians, particularly the Cherokees, normally grew several hundred acres of crops in each of their villages. By tradition, corn and beans were the staple crops, planted in hills four feet apart in four-foot rows. In between the corn hills were planted May apples. The Indians also grew potatoes, peas, pumpkins and gourds.

The "slash, burn and plant" Indian method of productively working the land was copied to good effect by the very adaptable Scots-Irish farmers, as they set down their roots and meticulously staked out territory they could call their own.

Apart from the horses, dogs and turkeys were the only domesticated animals to be found on an Indian reservation and most of the meat was supplied by hunting wild animals like buffalo in the plains and deer and bear in the forests that they roamed.

When the white settlers arrived into regions like South Western Virginia, North Carolina, East Tennessee and North Georgia in the second half of the 18th century, their first task was to erect a log cabin in a forest clearing before planting corn and raising a crop.

In most cases, the men initially came alone along rough pathways opened up for them by scouts and surveyors and, after setting up a homestead on an allotted space, they returned for their families and settled the following year.

The early settlers naturally showed a preference for tracts of land situated alongside the great rivers that bisected the Appalachian states, like the Ohio, the Cumberland, the Tennessee and the Mississippi. A ready supply of water in a region where summer climates were hot was an essential commodity and the farmlands at the river creeks were always the most productive.

East Tennessee historian Oliver Taylor recounts how when the first settlers cleared a piece of ground they invariably worked it until its producing quality was virtually exhausted. "They made no effort to restore the humus to the soil; they cleared and tilled a new piece while the old tract rested and reacted."

Some settler families were known to purchase or barter corn from Cherokee villages and most took their cue from the Indian methods of fishing and hunting buffalo, deer and bear, which supplied not just meat, but wool, hides, leather and sinews for cord.

The Indians and the white settlers were not always at each other's throats over ownership of territory and, in many areas, they recognised the mutual advantage of exchanging the particular material needs in each of their communities.

Horses, sheep, cattle and pigs helped supplement the income and improve the standard of living of the frontier settlers, who worked closely with their white settler neighbours from across the valley and further up the ridge and took refuge in communal forts on the occasions when attacks from hostile Indians were imminent.

The spirit of comradeship and dogged determination to survive within the white settler communities on the American frontier - of Scots-Irish, English and German - helped sustain a permanency to their land stakes in this vast and hitherto unchartered territory.

The Scots-Irish, however, were a more impetuous and restless people than the German and English settlers and, although many remained fixed when they made their first home, thousands of others felt the urge to move again and again.

It was often said at the time that no Scots-Irish family felt comfortable until they had moved twice. "They seem to have a psychological repugnance to making permanent homes until they found they had moved several times."

Feeder cattle, bred in the mountains by the frontier settlers, were sold when several years of age to farmers in East Tennessee, Virginia, Kentucky and Georgia. They were roughed through the winter, largely on corn stalks and wheat straw, fattened during the summer and autumn on clover pasture and grain, and driven painstakingly on foot along rough tracks to market in coastal cities like Philadelphia and Baltimore. The herding of hundreds of cattle and pigs over long stretches to market was a specialised job, with a fifteen-mile average day's travel to the markets for the farmers, their helpers and stock.

Employment could also be found in the corn mills, tanneries and blacksmith shops that acted as feeder industries to the farm communities and, as the years progressed, into the 19th century the prosperity of the rural townships and surrounding countryside improved considerably. It was relentless dawn to dusk toil with the rewards in hearth and home more material than monetary.

Land in the Appalachian backcountry was much cheaper than in the eastern seaboard states, with an average of five dollars an acre being fetched in Tennessee-Kentucky-Virginia-Georgia at the beginning of the 19th century, compared to a price of 50 dollars an acre in Pennsylvania, Maryland, New Jersey and New Hampshire.

Long before the advent of the plough and mechanised farm machinery, the main farm implements in the American backcountry were the rifle, axe, hoe, and sickle or scythe. Major changes were effected in agriculture during the mid-19th century when the horse-drawn reaper was invented by Virginia-born Cyrus McCormick, whose Presbyterian family emigrated a century before from Co Tyrone to the Shenandoah Valley.

In the early 18th century settlements, the settler and his wife had to make their own furniture, farm implements and clothing. Crude iron utensils were traded or purchased from the local blacksmiths.

The personal security of a frontier farmer and, that of his wife and their usually large family, depended primarily on him being a good shot with his trusted long rifle, and being fully observant to the potential dangers from man and beast that lurked behind almost every tree and hillside peak.

Frontier women had also to be strong and self-reliant. In addition to rearing a family and attending to the routine domestic chores about the home, they milked, gardened, cooked, carded the wool, spun the yarn and wove the thread into cloth on hand-made looms. The men may have called the shots in most aspects of frontier life, but the women were the backbone of family life, rearing the children and looking after the home.

Some of the proverbial sayings from folk on the frontier indicated a strong sense of inevitability in surroundings that for most of a century remained insecure:

• Never trouble trouble, until trouble troubles you.
• Do not argue with the wind.
• Today's today, and tomorrow's tomorrow.
• Come day, go day, God send Sunday.
• You can't rush God.

The routines and superstitions of frontier life endured with the seasons, with Sunday (The Sabbath) strictly set aside for worship and rest. The remainder of the week was for getting things done, materially and socially, although some thought Fridays and Saturdays were unlucky for tackling fresh enterprises.

President Andrew Jackson, a frontiersman in the traditional mould, never liked to begin anything of consequence on a Friday. He believed in leaving things off until the beginning of the week, which perhaps says more for the slower pace of life in those days.

Life was far from easy in the bleak wilderness landscape of the white frontier settlements, but the Scots-Irish, alongside the Germans, English, Scottish highlanders, French Huguenots, Welsh, and Scandinavians persevered, and together, as diverse peoples in a great melting pot, they left a rich cultural and social legacy that was to form the backbone of the American nation in the several hundred years that followed.

24

Money loaned for the *preservation of liberty and independence*

Few stories of the American War of Independence are as durable as the moral dilemma Ulster-born land-entry taker John Adair faced in 1779 at a crucial stage in hostilities between the revolutionaries and the British forces in the Appalachian back-country.

The intrepid Adair, a Presbyterian who originated from near Ballymena in Co Antrim and who lived for a time in Belfast before emigrating as an 18-year-old to America about 1770, was appointed land entry-taker for Sullivan county in North Carolina, now a part of Tennessee. His role was to collect the money for the state from the pioneering families who settled on tracts in this newly developed Watauga territory.

John Adair was a close friend and associate of the militia leaders Colonel Isaac Shelby and Colonel John Sevier, who were locally organising their expedition for the anticipated confrontation with the British redcoat forces led by Colonel Patrick Ferguson, from Aberdeen in Scotland.

Shelby and Sevier urgently needed money to finance the arming and equipping of their troops, and, with the farmers having invested all they had on the new lands, none was on hand or in prospect. The two colonels tried to borrow money on their own accounts, but they were unsuccessful and the only man circulating in the region with any substantial liquid cash was John Adair.

The problem was that the money - 12,735 dollars in total - did not belong to Adair; it was the property of the North Carolina state. But when approached by Shelby and Sevier his patriotism shone through and he readily agreed to a loan, on condition that it be fully repaid when the War was over.

Said Adair: "I have no authority in law to make that disposition of this money. It belongs to the impoverished treasury of North Carolina, and I dare not appropriate a cent of it to any purpose; but if our country is over-run by the British, our liberty is gone. Let the money go, too. Take it. If the enemy, by its use, is driven from the country, I can trust that country to justify and vindicate my conduct. So take it."

With the hard cash, ammunition and the necessary equipment was obtained for the Watauga militiamen, a large number of whom were pioneering Scots-Irish farmers and longhunters, and both Shelby and Sevier pledged that the money would be refunded in full, even out of their own pockets should the North Carolina legislature deem the action unlawful.

The militiamen routed Colonel Ferguson's troops at the Battle of Kings Mountain in October, 1780, in what was to be arguably the most decisive engagement of the Revolutionary War. And when it met in 1782, the North Carolina legislature accepted the action of the three men as totally appropriate on behalf of the people of the state.

John Adair, who lived in Sullivan county with his wife Ellen Crawford and family, served through the War as a volunteer in the militia and he acted as a scout, spying on Indian tribes in western Virginia. After the War, Adair received a 640-acre land grant in Knox county and he built Adair Station, a forted home about five miles from Knoxville.

By 1788, Adair was commissioner for purchasing supplies for the Cumberland Guard, which acted as armed escorts for travellers through the Tennessee wilderness via Nashville (Fort Nashborough) to the Cumberland plateau. He became a justice of the peace, a trustee of Blount College and the Hampden-Sidney Academy and served on the 1796 state constitutional convention in Knoxville which set down the founding principles for Tennessee.

John Adair was also a founding elder in First Knoxville Presbyterian Church along with fellow Scots-Irish pioneers James White and George McNutt. The first pastor of that church was the Rev Samuel Carrick, another Tennessee pioneer of Ulster extraction.

Adair died in 1827, aged 95, revered by his compatriots as a man who had courageously put himself out on a limb in pursuit of the liberty and independence of his people.

25

Pioneering road *to a new life*

The Great Wagon Road used by hundreds of thousands of 18th century Scots-Irish and other European ethnic settlers to push out the American frontiers was an ancient Indian path which started at Philadelphia and extended south through Maryland and Virginia into North Carolina, South Carolina, Georgia and Tennessee.

The Wagon Road - distance about 1,000 miles - was the first and, for a long time the only inter-colonial route in America. The only vehicular contact between the colonies and to the west was by this road or ships along the coast or a few navigable rivers. Some of the great battles in the Revolutionary War were fought in territory that ran alongside the Great Wagon Road and some of the fiercest militia campaigns against the native Indian tribes were conducted around the thoroughfare.

In the American Civil War of 1861-64 the Union and Confederate armies used this route, which today can be identified as covering broadly the same trans-Allegheny mountain territory where the modern United States inter-state highways 30, 81 and 11 occupy.

The Great Wagon Road has historically been compared with the Roman Appian Way in Europe of 2,000 years ago, for both its strategic military use and picturesque scenic beauty. Archaeologists says this was originally a pre-historic trail where buffalo, bear and other wild animals roamed freely. It was also known for centuries as a warpath for Iroquoian Indian tribes which included the five nations of the Cherokees, Tuscaroras, Siouans, Shawnees and Muskhogeans.

Towns and cities that grew up along the Great Wagon Road over a period of 100 years from the mid-18th century into the 19th century include Lancaster, York and Gettysburg (Pennsylvania); Harper's Ferry (West Virginia); Winchester, Newmarket, Harrisonburg, Staunton, Lexington, Roanoke and Rocky Mount (Virginia); Winston Salem, Salisbury and Charlotte (North Carolina); Camden, Newberry and Columbia (South Carolina) and Augusta (Georgia).

A chronicler of early Tennessee vividly recalls the days of the Great Wagon Road from Pennsylvania: "The early occupants of cabins were among the most happy of mankind. Exercise and excitement gave them health; they were practically equal; common danger made them mutually dependent; brilliant hopes of future wealth and distinction led them on; and as there was ample room for all, and as each newcomer increased individual and general security, there was little room for that envy, jealousy and hatred which constitute a large portion of human misery in older societies.

"Never were the story, the song and the laugh better enjoyed than upon the hewed blocks, or puncheon stools, around the roaring log fire of the early western settlers who moved along the Great Wagon Road."

The Eastern Pennsylvania-built Conestoga wagon, with its distinctive structure, was a feature of daily life on the Great Wagon Road, carrying the Scots-Irish, English and German settlers from one point to the next over the ever widening stretch of frontier. Built with its sides sloping inward like a well-made boat, the wagon held its cargo firmly in place no matter how rough the terrain of the Great Wagon Road might be.

The wagons reached a length of twenty-six feet and a height of eleven and normally it took six heavy horses to pull it. At the time of the Revolutionary War a Conestoga wagon capable of moving a family with belongings cost 250 dollars, with an additional 1,200 dollars required to purchase the horses.

• Reliable examinations by American historians of Revolutionary War pension lists, muster rolls and census papers at the end of the 18th century confirmed that in North Carolina and Tennessee, the English and the Scots-Irish were each about one-third of the population; in Kentucky, the English were 40 per cent and the Scots-Irish 30 per cent, and in Georgia, English and Scots-Irish were each about 40 per cent of all names. German settlers accounted for one-fifth of settlers in North Carolina, one-seventh in Tennessee and one-twelfth in Kentucky.

26

Scots-Irish *in the Chattahoochee territory*

Rabun county in the wooded mountainous terrain of north west Georgia close to the Tennessee, North Carolina and South Carolina state boundaries became a stronghold for Scots-Irish families in the early 19th century and today many residents of the region remain intensely proud of these ethnic roots.

Many of the first Rabun county settlers moved from South and North Carolina after their parents and grandparents had trekked through the Shenandoah Valley of Virginia from Pennsylvania or headed up into the Piedmont region from the port of Charleston.

Georgia was sparsely populated at the time of the Revolutionary war. In 1753, its population was less than 2,400 and the movement of families from Virginia and the Carolinas did not begin in earnest until 1773, when the then Governor Wright purchased a large tract of land in mid-Georgia between the Savannah and Oconee rivers.

Soldiers and Indian traders were the first white men to inhabit the fairly isolated 900,000-acre Chattahoochee forest region and the initial batch of families drifted in during the years after land treaties with the native tribes were completed in 1785 by Revolutionary War officer General Andrew Pickens, whose parents Andrew and Nancy Davis Pickens emigrated from Ulster to Pennsylvania in the 1720s.

The attraction of new land, even in upland country, brought the Scots-Irish and English families to Rabun county and, with the new American nation gradually emerging from the ravages of war and extending out west beyond its recognised boundaries, the target of these pioneering settlers was primarily to improve their economic conditions.

Andrew Pickens, who married Rebecca Calhoun, a cousin of the leading South Carolina statesman and American Vice-President John C. Calhoun, was a veteran of the French-Indian Wars of 1754-63. He was awarded a sword and was made a brigadier general by act of the American Congress for his valour at the Battle of Cowpens in 1781.

Later, Pickens led militia in a decisive battle against the Cherokee Indians in the Little Tennessee Valley, on the site of present-day Rabun county. The battle is still vividly remembered in Rabun county folklore and the highest mountain, Picken's Nose, is named in memory of the formidable general, who is buried at Tamasee, just across the Chattanooga River.

It was only after the Cherokee Indians were driven out of what is now Rabun county towards the Mississippi river basin that the white settlers moved into the region with any real sense of security and long-term stake.

One who led the way was John Dillard, who acquired four lots of land of 250 acres each in the centre of the Little Tennessee Valley. Dillard served with General Andrew Pickens in the Revolutionary War and in the various expeditions against the Cherokees and today Rabun county boasts a large population of his kinsfolk.

The settlement was gradual and the census of 1820 shows that only 524 were living in Rabun county, which was set up by the Georgia legislature the previous year. By 1830, the population had increased to 2,176.

Those who were living in the county before it was officially established had no title to the land on which they lived except what permission they might have had from the Indians or from Georgia state agents who patrolled the area in the period when the tribes were moving away. Most of the county "squatters" were eventually awarded legal rights to their land.

The county was named after William Rabun, governor of Georgia at the time, and the main town in the settlement was Clayton, today with a population of 3,000. Land in this fairly inaccessible mountain country was allocated by the drawing of lots and the tracts were paired off to encompass 250 acres each.

The modest land speculators who comprised a significant sprinkling of Scots-Irish settlers from down-state Georgia or the neighbouring South Carolina Piedmont invested at one dollar an acre, but the rougher less productive stretches went for much lower prices on a "sight unseen" basis. Lots of several hundred acres in the rougher "bad land" districts were bought for sums as low as 25 dollars.

Corn growing and livestock production were the main outlets for farmers in the region, but, for many, life was continually a struggle on the rough hilly land.

During the American Civil War there were not enough men left in the Confederate stronghold of Rabun county to produce enough corn to make bread. In 1863, the Georgia legislature was forced to enact laws for the relief of families of men in service and inflated Confederate currency made it almost impossible to obtain sugar, salt and coffee.

Moonshining, or illicit poteen-making, a practice prevalent in Scots-Irish up-country communities, has long been a tradition for some in Rabun county, just as it was for several centuries in the hills and valleys of south-eastern Pennsylvania, south-western Virginia, West Virginia, East Tennessee, and eastern Kentucky.

By and large, however, Rabun county has always been a tightly-knit, law-abiding and God-fearing society with the accepted modes of living set as high as in any similar-sized rural American community. Indeed, firm foundations on law-enforcement and church observance were laid by the pioneering first Rabun settlers.

The Bleckleys were a leading Rabun county family from the start. They were of mixed Scots-Irish, English and German Lutheran stock and had reached North Georgia via Virginia and North Carolina.

James Bleckley, a noted Indian fighter, was a man of humble background and, while initially not a landowner, he was in the county at the very beginning and played a greater part than almost any other man in getting things up and running. He became the county's first court sheriff and a son Logan E. Bleckley was chief justice and considered one of Georgia's most eminent jurists.

The Ritchie family of Rabun county are descended from Alexander Ritchie (Richey) and wife Jane Caldwell, who along with other Scotch-Irish families emigrated from Ulster to Pennsylvania in 1727 and first settled at Lancaster and Chester counties.

The Ritchie and Caldwell families moved to Virginia. before setting up home at Abbeville in South Carolina. Eli Ritchie, a great grandson of the original pioneers, owned land at Macon county in North Carolina and he eventually he extended this to 975 acres in the Little Tennessee Valley of Rabun county. Eli was a militia soldier in the Creek War of 1812.

The McKinneys were another prominent early Scots-Irish family in the Little Tennessee Valley, with William and Peggy McKinney and their children moving from Buncombe county in North Carolina.

The McClains, of Rabun county, can be traced to Captain John McClain, a Carolina company commander in the Revolutionary War, and his wife Mary Ann McNair. John's long military service earned him a 80 dollars a year pension and entitled him to an extensive tract of land in Georgia.

Other Scots-Irish families in first Rabun county settlements were the McConnells, McDowells, McCurrys, Millers and McClures. While most families in the county are descended from English, north of Ireland and Scottish settlers, a few are of German and Dutch Lutheran and French Huguenot extraction.

The Baptists were the first to officially organise churches in the county, followed by the Methodists, in the wake of the camp meeting revivals of the early 1800s, and Presbyterians, traditionally linked to the Scots-Irish. Down the years, Rabun county has had little or no Episcopal or Roman Catholic church presence.

This rugged north west Georgia county is typical of many rural Appalachian regions where 18th and early 19th century Scots-Irish settlers were amongst the first inhabitants.

Logo of Rabun County, Georgia.

27

Mountain railroad dream *of an enterprising Ulsterman*

The Blue Ridge Mountain region was settled by many Scots-Irish families in the late 18th century and early 19th century, including the family of John C. Calhoun, whose father Patrick emigrated from Co Donegal and settled at Abbeville in the Carolina Piedmont.

A Blue Ridge Mountain railroad was an innovative concept spearheaded by John C. Calhoun, but financial, logistical and political difficulties over a period of 50 years prevented it from being fully accomplished. The outbreak of the American Civil War in 1861 proved to be the deathknell for a highly ambitious project that would have provided a major economic boost to a still embryonic frontier region.

Part of the line was completed from the port of Charleston to Walhalla in Georgia and even after the Civil War, the remainder of the Blue Ridge Mountain railroad to its ultimate destination of the Ohio River was still being pursued as a viable concept by leading citizens in the region, but as time passed and other arterial routes were opened up through Appalachia to the west it became much more of a dream than a reality.

Remarkably, the John C. Calhoun-inspired railroad was proposed at a time when there were only 1,000 miles of rail track in the whole United States and the grand idea was to serve a highly undeveloped mountainous area by linking Charleston on the Atlantic coast in South Carolina to Cincinnati on the Ohio River.

The railroad would have embraced the states of South Carolina, North Carolina, Georgia, Tennessee, Kentucky and Ohio and the charter for the work was granted by the Georgia legislature in 1838. The cost of the initial capital stock for the railroad in Georgia alone was estimated at 1,700,000 dollars and collecting books were even issued in the Georgian cities of Augusta and Athens.

In those days, the erection of a railroad over such a long stretch of territory was an awesome task. There were no great machines for moving material as we have today. All movement of dirt had to be done with dump carts and wheel barrows. All drilling of rock was done by hand with hammer and steel. Great cuts had to be dug out of the sides of mountains. It took an army of men to slowly prepare the ground and methodically lay the tracks.

John C. Calhoun first advocated a railroad through the Blue Ridge country when a young member of the South Carolina legislature in the 1820s and he continued to actively back the idea during his long service in Washington as Congressman, Senator, Secretary of War and Vice-President during two terms.

Calhoun was a scion of genuine Scots-Irish stock with strong Christian values, work ethic, integrity and enterprise. His personal initiative and drive in attempting to push a railroad through the Blue Ridge country via his own town of Clemson in the South Carolina Piedmont was part of a great dream. But the indomitable Calhoun died in 1850, with his mountain railroad objective still in the melting pot, far from reality.

The Blue Ridge Railroad employed up to 2,000 people before the Civil War and its rapid demise in the years after led to considerable social and economic decline in the region.

• President Andrew Jackson, whom John C. Calhoun served under as Vice-President, was the first American President to travel by railroad. On June 6, 1833, he travelled on the Baltimore-Ohio railroad from Ellicot's Mills, Maryland to Baltimore.

28

Scots-Irish *dialect and speech*

" Scotch-Irish speech" in the United States is a dialect that can be located in the Appalachian and Ozark mountain region, the lower Mississippi Valley, Texas and the Southern Plains. It has been spoken in America for more than 250 years and has even permeated in the manner of speaking of other ethic groups in the south eastern highland country.

Back in 1772, a newspaper advertisement reported a runaway black slave named Jack who was said to "speak Scotch-Irish dialect." Such was the speech and dialect of the white population that the enslaved African Americans very often aped the speech play of their masters.

The speech is distinctive for its patterns of pronunciation, with usage of whar for where, thar for there, hard for hire, winder for window, widder for widow, and narrer for narrow.

The Scots-Irish of the Appalachian region also had their own distinctive vocabulary in words such as: fornenst (next to), nigh (near), swan (swear), skift (dusting of snow), fixin' (getting ready to do something), hant (ghost), lettin' on (pretending). scawmy (misty), brickle (brittle), bumfuzzled (confused) and scoot (slide).

In many parts of the Appalachian region the colloquial language has remained virtually unchanged for several hundred years, with very often a saltliness added to the dialect. Scots-Irish influences have rubbed off on Appalachian characteristics in many ways, with language and dialect probably the most traceable link to the 18th century first frontier settlements.

Buried with dignity

Second generation Ulsterman John C. Calhoun, who was vice-president of the United States for two terms and a most influential early leader of the American South, was one of the first to be buried in a Fisk-made coffin in 1850.

Calhoun's coffin greatly impressed many of the country's leaders of the day including Jefferson Davis, Henry Clay and Daniel Webster that they wrote a letter in which the new type metallic casket was declared to be "the best article known to us for transporting the dead to their final resting place."

A Fisk coffin had a viewing glass and stories of people being buried alive were legendary, with some speculating that the glass covering may have been for the purpose of detecting "a breath" on the glass , or any eye movement.

New York inventor Almond D. Fisk, however, emphasised the air-tight aspect of the casket and its ability to preserve the body for weeks, months and even years.

The metal casket, with the lid securely fastened, was also promoted as a means of thwarting grave robbers — who were very active at the time.

29

They said *of the Scots-Irish*

"The Scots-Irish who came to America in the 18th century had a pride which was a source of irritation to their English neighbours. It was said of a Scots-Irish man that his looks spoke out that he would not fear the devil should he meet him face to face".

Sketches of the Some of the First Settlers of Upper Georgia
by George R. Gilmer.

"Whole neighbourhoods formed parties for removal so that departure from their native country is no longer exile. He that goes thus accompanied . . . sits down in a better climate, surrounded by his kindred and his friends; they carry with them their language, their opinions, their popular songs and hereditary merriment: they change nothing but the place of their abode."

Dr Samuel Johnson on the emigration from Britain to America, 1773.

"The history of the Scotch-Irish is necessarily a history of the troubles they suffered on account of their religion. The great principles of religious liberty were not recognised in the seventeenth and the early part of the eighteenth century."

Joseph A. Waddell, in his History of Augusta County, Virginia.

"It is a fact that the Irish emigrants and their children are now in possession of the government of Pennsylvania, by their majority in the Assembly, as well as of the great part of the territory: and I remember well the first ship that brought any of them over."

Benjamin Franklin in 1784 on Scots-Irish control of
Pennsylvania government.

"The Scotch-Irish were marked by family loyalty. The women led hard lives, but were patient and submission, and submerged in the status of their husbands."

Arthur W. Calhoun, descendant of John C. Calhoun,
in his book The American Family - The Colonial Period.

"Inquiries as to family history and racial stock rarely bring a more definite answer than that grandparents or great-grandparents came from North Carolina or Virginia or occasionally from Pennsylvania, and that they 'reckon' their folks were 'English,' 'Scotch,' or 'Irish,' any of which designations may mean Scotch-Irish."

John C. Campbell, The Southern Highlander and his Homeland.

"My father was a man of practical judgement, and of great industry and perseverence . . . he was a kind father, a sincere friend, and an honest and religious man."

President James Buchanan on his father Patrick, who emigrated
to America from Co Donegal in 1789. Patrick Buchanan
was typical of a great many of the Presbyterian
immigrants from Ulster.

"The early Scots-Irish settlers were the true frontiersmen who carried the rifle, the axe, and the Bible everywhere they went, happy and proud to be secure in their own lands and free to have churches of their own choice."

South Carolina historian FitzHugh McMaster.

"The Scotch-Irish person seems to have been paradoxical. He has been described as both venturesome and cautious, taciturn to a fault, but speaking his mind freely when aroused. Eventually serious, he could nevertheless display a sense of humor; fondness for sports revealed his sociability. Friend and foe alike were objects of his steadfast attention and his nature rebelled against anything that savored of injustice or deceit, nor did it take kindly to restraint of any kind. The Scotch-Irish character - prompt to resist an affront, unrelenting to foes - was to leave an imprint on the history of the Revolutionary War."

Wilma Dykeman, south eastern American mountain country historian.

THE SCOTS-IRISH CHRONICLES
by Billy Kennedy

The Scots-Irish in the Hills of Tennessee
(First published 1995)

Centred in Tennessee, this book is the definite story of how the American frontier of the late 18th century was advanced and the indomitable spirit of the Scots-Irish shines through on every page. From the Great Smoky Mountain region to the Cumberland Plateau and the Mississippi River delta region, the Scots-Irish created a civilisation out of a wilderness. The inheritance they left was hard-won, but something to cherish.

The Scots-Irish in the Shenandoah Valley
(First published 1996)

The beautiful Shenandoah Valley alongside the majestic backdrop of the Blue Ridge Mountains of Virginia is the idyllic setting for the intriguing story of a brave resolute people who tamed the frontier. The Ulster-Scots were a breed of people who could move mountains. They did this literally with their bare hands in regions like the Shenandoah Valley, winning the day for freedom and   liberty of conscience in the United States.

The Scots-Irish in the Carolinas
(First published 1997)

The Piedmont areas of the Carolina region, North and South, were settled by   tens of thousands of Scots-Irish Presbyterians in the second half of the 18th century. Some moved down the Great Wagon Road from Pennsylvania, others headed to the up-country after arriving at the port of Charleston. The culture, political heritage and legacy of the Scots-Irish so richly adorn the fabric of American life and the Carolinas was an important homeland for many of these people. It was also the launching pad for the long trek westwards to new lands and the fresh challenge of the expanding frontier.

The Scots-Irish in Pennsylvania and Kentucky
(First published 1998)

Pennsylvania and Kentucky are two American states settled primarily at opposite ends of the 18th century by Ulster-Scots Presbyterians, yet this book details how the immigrant trail blended in such diverse regions. A common thread runs through Pennsylvania, Virginia, North Carolina, South Carolina, Tennessee, West Virginia, Georgia, Kentucky and other neighbouring states - that of a settlement of people who had firmly set their faces on securing for all time - their Faith and Freedom.

These books are available from authorised booksellers in the United Kingdom, the United States and the Republic of Ireland or direct from the publisher.

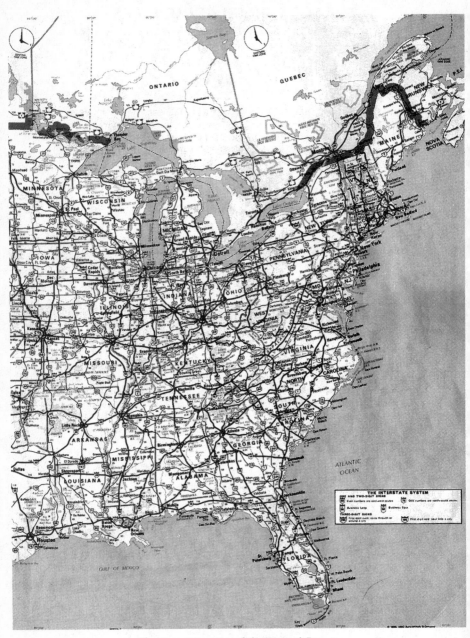

The eastern states of the United States.

30

An American's *view*

The year was 1780 and the people of what is now north-east Tennessee found themselves threatened by the war raging on the other side of the Allegheny Mountains. The inhabitants of this sparsely populated wilderness area were predominantly Scotch - Irish, with a sprinkling of Germans and French Huguenots, as well as native Americans.

These were pioneers - "back country" people - fiercely independent, and in many ways unlike the colonists of the seaboard plantations.

The American revolution was blazing from the coast to the eastern slopes of the mountains of Virginia, North and South Carolina and Georgia, but the people of the mountains and valleys of the Watauga and French Broad, among other western rivers, had little interest in the war. That would soon change.

Lieutenant Colonel Patrick Ferguson, a Highland Scot by birth in Aberdeen, commanded British and loyalist forces on the eastern side of the Alleghenies. Ferguson sent word to the colonists that unless they joined him and fought for the Crown he would march over the mountains and destroy their settlements - "with fire and sword."

Ferguson chose an inflammatory phrase to challenge the Scotch-Irish. The words "with fire and sword" were used by Scottish forces loyal to the English Crown as early as 1644 when the McDonalds had supported King Charles 1 and had threatened to ravage the territory around Loch Etive "with fire and sword." This direct challenge enraged the freedom-loving Scotch-Irish of the American highlands

and, instead of terrorising them, it propelled them to take up arms —
against Patrick Ferguson and his troops.

Word was sent that all able-bodied men should muster at Sycamore
Shoals on the Watauga River at the site of present-day Elizabethton,
Tennessee. After electing officers, the citizen-soldiers marched to
Kings Mountain on the North Carolina-South Carolina border where
they met Ferguson with "fire and sword" on October 7, 1780.

Led by Colonel William Campbell, among others, the American
militiamen surrounded and engaged Ferguson's force made up of
1,100 regular British troops and Tories from the Carolinas. Attired in
hunting shirts and armed with long rifles and belt axes, the 1,000-plus
"mountain men" trapped and defeated the loyalists, killing a large
number, including Lieutenant Colonel Ferguson, whose cairn can still
be seen on the battlefield today.

Kings Mountain is recognised as one of the decisive battles and a
major turning point in the American revolution. The British soon
abandoned their efforts to subdue the Southern colonies, due in part to
their defeat at Kings Mountain and the subsequent defeat at nearby
Cowpens in January, 1781 and to the fact that Patrick Ferguson had
served as linchpin of that effort. No one ever dared to cross those
mountains again and face the wrath of the Scotch-Irish riflemen.

TOMMY RYE,
Maryville, East Tennessee.

Author's *acknowledgments*

- John Rice Irwin, Museum of Appalachia, Norris, Tennessee
- H. David Wright, Gallatin, Tennessee
- Tommy Rye, Maryville, Tennessee
- Dean McMakin, St Charles, Illinois
- Glenn M. Brady, Zachary, Louisiana
- George Gilmore, Aghadowey, Co Londonderry
- Cherel Henderson, East Tennessee Historical Society, Knoxville
- Dr Charles Moffatt, Gallatin, Tennessee
- Kent Redgrave, Nashville, Tennessee
- Emily Yarborough, Maryville College, Tennessee
- Councillor Dr Ian Adamson, Belfast
- John Lebert, Knoxville, Tennessee
- Fred Brown, Knoxville News Sentinel, Tennessee
- Senator Strom Thurmond, Washington DC
- Barbara A. Wolanin, Curator, The Architect of the Capitol, Washington DC
- Tom Evans, National Graphic Center, Falls Church, Virginia
- Mary Elizabeth Law, Rabun County Historical Society, Clayton, Georgia
- Myron Allen, Salem, South Carolina
- Stevan Jackson, Jonesborough, Tennessee
- Barbara Parker, Department of Tourist Development, Nashville
- Eileen Crawford, Divinity School Library, Vanderbilt University, Nashville
- Thomas T. Barber, Thomasville, North Carolina

Pictures *and illustrations*

- National Graphic Center, Falls Church, Virginia
- H. David Wright, Gallatin, Tennessee
- George Gilmore, Aghadowey, Co Londonderry
- John Rice Irwin, Museum of Appalachia, Norris, Tennessee
- Maryville College, Blount County Tennessee
- Upper Octorara Presbyterian Church, Pennsylvania
- The National Trust, Northern Ireland
- Tennessee Historical Society
- East Tennessee Historical Society, Knoxville
- Religion in Tennessee 1777-1945 by Herman A. Norton
- Paths of the Past by Paul H. Bergeron
- Rabun County Historical Society, Georgia
- The Complete Book of United States Presidents by William A. Degregorio
- National Portrait Gallery, Smithsonian Institution

Bibliography *and references consulted*

- History of Greater Wheeling and Vicinity by Charles A. Wingerter
- History of the Pan-Handle, West Virginia by J. H. Newton
- Two Hundred and Fifty Years at Upper Octorara
- Presbyterians in the South (Volume 1) by Ernest Trice Thompson
- The Great Wagon Road by Frederick and Maxine Newbraugh
- Religion in Tennessee 1777-1945 by Herman A. Norton
- Paths of the Past: Tennessee 1770-1970 by Paul H. Bergeron
- Sketch of the Old Scotch Church Settlement at Union Church, Natchez, Mississippi
- Cultural Pre-Adaptation and the Upland South by Milton Newton, Louisiana State University, Baton Rouge
- My Life and Sacred Songs by Ira D. Sankey
- The Revolutionary College: American Presbyterian Higher Education 1707-1837 by Howard Miller
- History of New Providence Presbyterian Church (Maryville, Tennessee) by Will A. McTeer
- Nor Principalities Nor Powers - A History (1621-1991) of First Carrickfergus Presbyterian Church by D. J. McCartney
- A Century of Maryville College (Tennessee) by Samuel Tyndale Wilson
- By Faith Endowed - The Story of Maryville College by Carolyn L. Blair and Arda S. Walker
- Historic Sullivan County, Tennessee by Oliver Taylor
- The Scotch-Irish: A Social History by James G. Leyburn
- One of Those Tall Tennesseans (The life of G. S. W. Crawford) by Earle W. Crawford
- America's First Western Frontier: East Tennessee by Brenda C. Calloway
- Samuel Doak by Earle W. Crawford

- Stories of the Great West by Theodore Roosevelt
- Houston and Crockett: Heroes of Tennessee and Texas, An Anathology
- The Minnis Family: Blount County Pioneers by Jane Kizer Thomas
- West Nashville: Its People and Environs
- Albion's Seed by David Hackett Fischer
- The Presbyterian Church in South Carolina
- Memoirs of Rev Isaac Anderson by Rev John J. Robinson
- Patriots of Kings Mountain by Dr Bobby Gilmer Moss
- Memoir of Rev Isaac Anderson by Rev J. Robinson
- The Encyclopedia of the South by Robert O'Brien
- Tennessee Music: Its People and Its Places by Peter Coats Zimmerman
- The Complete Book of US Presidents by William A. Degregorio
- First Families of Tennessee (East Tennessee Historical Society)
- Sweet Believing (Character Studies of the Scottish Covenanters) by Jock Purves
- Ulster Emigration to Colonial America by R. J. Dickson
- First Families of Tennessee (East Tennessee Historical Society)
- The French Broad-Holston Country by Mary U. Rothrock
- Alex Stewart - Portrait of a Pioneer by John Rice Irwin
- An Historical Sketch of the Presbyterian Synod of Tennessee
- The Great Wagon Road by Parke Rouse Jun.
- The New Bethel Church Sesquicentennial
- Kingsport Heritage: The Early Years by Muriel M. C. Spoden
- The Catheys of Marshall County, Tennessee
- David Crockett - The Man Behind the Myth by James Wakefield Burke
- Davy Crockett - The Man, The Legend, The Legacy by Michael A. Lofaro
- Tennesseans At War by James A. Crutchfield
- Old Frontiers by John P. Brown
- Valley So Wild: A Folk History by Alberta and Carson Brewer
- Sketches of Rabun County History 1819-1948 by Andrew Jackson Ritchie
- Rabun County, Georgia and Its People, Volume 1
- Almost Heaven: Travels Through the Backwoods of America by Martin Fletcher
- The Overmountain Men by Pat Alderman
- Highlanders in America by John Patterson MacLean
- With Fire and Sword (The Battle of Kings Mountain) by Wilma Dykeman
- Faithful Volunteers: The History of Religion in Tennessee by Stephen Mansfield and George Grant

Index

G

Gallagher - Rev James 53, 141. James 82.
Sarah 82
Gamble - Josias 82. Ann 82, Robert (11) 82,
91, 92. Mary 82, 91, 92. John 91
Gambill - Martin 92
Garfield - President James A. 140
Gault - William 79
Gass - Jacob 82. Mary 82. John 82. Margaret
82. Samuel 83, 96. Rebecca 83, 96
Gaut - John Sen. 83. Letitia 83
George - King (111) 74
George - King (11) 154
Ghormley - Abraham 83, 92. Elizabeth 83,
92. Hugh 92. Catherine 92. Samuel 92.
Joseph 92. Jasper 92. Michael 92. Jesse 92
Gilbreath - Hugh 83, 92, 93. Elizabeth 83, 92.
John Fisher 93
Gillespie - George 83, 93. Elizabeth 83, 93.
George 93. Ann 93. Robert Neilson 93. James
93. Jennet 93. John 93. James Jun. 93.
William 93. John Jun. 93. Dr James Houston
93
Gilmer - George R. 177
Glass - William 83, 94. Sarah 83, 94
Glendenin - James 64
Gloucester - John 56
Goldsmith - Oliver 143
Graham - Rev William 48, 49
Grant - President Ulysses Simpson 108, 139,
140
Grant - Joseph 16
Gregg - James 39. James 75. Robert 83.
Lydia Alice 83
Guthery - Adam 83

H

Halliday - Samuel 14
Hamilton - James Sen. 83
Hancock - John 14
Harden - Francis 75
Harrison - President Benjamin 112, 139, 140
Hartford - John 126
Half King - Chief 29
Hearst - John 40. Elizabeth 40
Hill - Aaron 16
Hines - William 83. Martha 83
Hogan - Humphrey 64

Hogue - Moses 49
Holston - Stephen 63
Hoss - Bishop E. E. 77
Houston - Samuel 55, 56. Elizabeth 55.
Samuel Sen. 55. James 55. James 83, 94.
Agnes 83, 94. John 83, 95. Sarah 83, 95.
Samuel 83. Elizabeth 83. Robert 87.
Margaret 95. Rev Samuel 95
Hoyt - Rev Darius 56. Rev Ard 56
Hughes - David 83. Anna 83
Humphries - Dr William 143
Humphrey - William 83, Sarah 83
Hutcheson - Frances 14

I

Inglis - Rev Dr Charles 47
Irwin - John Rice 9, 10, 11, James 112

J

Jackson - Andrew 7, 20, 22, 43, 56, 90, 103,
116, 117, 123, 132, 133, 135, 139, 140, 141,
142, 143, 144, 149, 150, 151,156, 174.
Thomas Jonathan 50. Rachel Donelson 140,
143. Elizabeth 7, 141, 142. Andrew Sen. 7
James - King (1) 22. King (11) 23
Jefferson - Thomas 14
Johnson - Henry 83. Rachel 83. President
Andrew 116, 139, 140. Eliza McCardle 140.
Daniel 155. Dr Samuel 177
Johnston - John B. Sen. 83. Elizabeth 83
Junkin - Dr George 50, 51. Eleanor 50.
Margaret 50

K

Kelly - Alexander 83, 95. Nancy 83, 95. John
84, 95, 96. Margaret 84
Kennedy - Rev James 84, 96. Mary Jane 84.
Dr Samuel 84. Rebeckah Meek 84, 96. David
114
Kerr - David 96
Kilgore - Charles 84. Winnie 84
Kinkead - David 158. Joseph 158. Winnifred
158
King - Henry 84. Sarah 84
Knox - John 21, 41
Kyle - Robert 84. Leah 84

Scots-Irish lectures delivered in United States by the author : 1994-1999

Tennessee:
* Middle Tennessee State University, Murfreesboro.
* East Tennessee State University, Johnson City
* Belmont University, Nashville
* Rotary Club, Morristown
* King's Presbyterian College, Bristol
* The Hermitage, Nashville
* East Tennessee Historical Society, Knoxville
* Chatanooga Historical Society
* Tolahoma Historical Society
* Sycamore Shoals State Historic Park, Elizabethton
* Murfreesboro Highland Games
* Scottish Association, Knoxville
* Davis Kidd Book Stores, Knoxville and Nashville
* Rotary Club, Rogersville
* Maryville College, Blount County
* Museum of Appalachia, Norris

Virginia:
* Museum of American Frontier Culture, Staunton
* Ferrum College
* The Bookery, Lexington
* Grayson County Historical Society, Independence
* Abingdon Historical Society
* Book Store, Charlottesville

Kentucky:
* Berea College, Berea
* Barnes and Noble Book Store, Louisville

South Carolina:
* Clemson University
* McCormick County Historical Society
* Donalds Historical Society, Abbeville
* Erskine Theological Seminary
* South Carolina Historical Round Table, Greenville
* Gaffney College
* Barnes and Noble Book Stores, Greenville and Spartanburg

North Carolina:
* Historical Society, Franklin
* Barnes and Noble Book Store, Charlotte
* Books A Million Store, Asheville
* Andrew Jackson Centre, Waxhaws
* Appalachian Conference, Boone
* Historical Society, Waynesville

Pennsylvania:
* Scotch-Irish Society of United States, Philadelphia
* Elizabethton College
* Donegal Presbyterian Church, Lancaster County
* First Pittsburgh Presbyterian Church
* Historical Cultural Centre, Winter's House, Elizabethton